# DISCIPLING THE FLOCK

## A CALL TO FAITHFUL SHEPHERDING

Paul Tautges

COUNSEL FOR THE HEART

A RESOURCE for WORD-BASED TRANSFORMATION and PRACTICAL DISCIPLESHIP

*Discipling the Flock—A Call to Faithful Shepherding*

First published in 2009 as *Counsel Your Flock*

ISBN:
Print: 978-1-63342-142-4
Mobi: 978-1-63342-144-8
ePub: 978-1-63342-143-1

Published by Shepherd Press
P.O. Box 24
Wapwallopen,
Pennsylvania 18660

eBooks: www.shepherdpress.com/ebooks



BP 22 21 20 19 18 17 16 15

Library of Congress Cataloging-in-Publication Data

Names: Tautges, Paul, author.
Title: Discipling the flock : a call to faithful shepherding / Paul Tautges.
Other titles: Counsel your flock
Description: Wapwallopen, PA : Shepherd Press, 2018. | Originally published:

Counsel your flock. Leominster, England : Day One Publications, 2009. |
Includes bibliographical references.
Identifiers: LCCN 2018017079| ISBN 9781633421424 (trade pbk. : alk. paper) |

ISBN 9781633421431 (epbu)
Subjects: LCSH: Discipling (Christianity) | Pastoral theology. | Pastoral counseling.
Classification: LCC BV4520 .T38 2018 | DDC 153--dc23 LC record available at https://lccn.loc.gov/2018017079

Cover Design by Andy Heckathorne, http://andyheckathorne.com/
Design and Typesetting by Caroline McCausland
Printed in the United States of America

# ENDORSEMENTS

A gathering storm surrounds the day in which we live, a dark hour in which the absolute sufficiency of the Scripture has come under attack. But how refreshing–and rare–to see a book like this that asserts the irresistible power of God's Word to develop true discipleship by the sovereign working of His Spirit. This is not a 'trendy book' like so many, blown about by the prevailing evangelical winds. Rather, here is an anchor for authentic ministry that will stimulate real spiritual growth in God's people. May the Lord set an open door before this book and use it to affect the lives of many.

Dr. Steven J. Lawson, President, OnePassion Ministries; speaker; and author of many books, including *Famine in the Land, The Expository Genius of John Calvin,* and *Foundations of Grace*

This book is excellent! Grounded in the Scriptures and framed by the gospel, it addresses both the pastor and pastoral ministry. The pastor is to "watch his life and doctrine closely." And from this vital foundation, the pastor is to "shepherd the flock of God under your care." Tautges addresses both of these matters, and he does so as one understands it from his role on the front-lines of pastoral ministry. I recommend you read this masterful little book twice. Read it first through the lens of the pastor. Read it a second time through the lens of the people of God. And in the second read, invite your elders to read it with you.

Greg Strand, Executive Director of Biblical Theology and Credentialing, Interim Director of Pastoral Care Ministries, EFCA; Adjunct Professor of Pastoral Theology at Trinity Evangelical Divinity School

In this companion to his previous book, **Counseling One Another**, Paul Tautges makes it clear that for this one-another ministry to take place, it is essential that pastors and elders understand the key role that they play in the discipleship process. Believers need a way to measure their leaders' discipleship philosophy and skills, and leaders need a way to teach them to be involved in the counseling, discipleship, restoring-one-another ministry. This is a book about local-church discipleship, of which leadership is a big part. **Discipling the Flock** addresses an important need. This is a must-read!

Dr. Ron Allchin, Executive Director of the Biblical Counseling Center in Arlington Heights, Illinois

This book gets it right! Comprehensive and convincing, **Discipling the Flock** shows how true biblical counseling and preaching fit hand-in-glove. Those who preach, teach, or counsel regularly are sure to benefit greatly from this helpful resource.

Dr. John MacArthur, Pastor-Teacher of Grace Community Church in Sun Valley, California

Many men go to seminary to learn how to preach sermons, not shepherd individual souls or train congregations to counsel. As long as a pastor can preach a good sermon he is well equipped to pastor a church. But not only does this concept of pastoral ministry violate the discipleship ministry of the New Testament church (Acts 20:20, 31; Col. 1:28–29), it is also a wrong view of preaching ... One-on-one counseling is one form of proclaiming or preaching the Word other than the proclamation of the Word from a pulpit.

Dr. John D. Street, Chair, Graduate Program in Biblical Counseling, The Master's University and Seminary, Santa Clarita, California

Too many pastors focus solely on their preaching while others neglect it in the name of discipleship. There is a needed voice to help pastors today realize both are essential to a faithful long-term ministry. You hold in your hands a biblically faithful, practically helpful guide to find the important balance between the public and private ministry of the Word of God in a local church. I commend this book and the author's faithful example of it in his own ministry.

Brian Croft, Senior Pastor, Auburndale Baptist Church; Founder of Practical Shepherding; and Senior Fellow, Church Revitalization Center, SBTS

Dedication

To Victor Simeonovich Ryagusov, pastor of Transfiguration Church in Samara, Russia, whose example and steadfast commitment to church-based leadership training are paving the way for a new generation of teaching shepherds in the former Soviet Union

# A WORD OF THANKS

I thank Victor Simeonovich Ryagusov, pastor of Transfiguration Church in Samara, for his grace, perseverance, and unwavering vision for the establishment of church-based preachers' institutes so that biblical expositors may become fruitful and multiply throughout the land of Russia. May their tribe increase! "Preach the word; be ready in season and out of season; reprove, rebuke, exhort, with great patience and instruction" (2 Tim. 4:2).

I thank Jim Holmes for insisting that I radically trim down my initial manuscript, which became another book, *Counseling One Another*, thus allowing this smaller book to be directed more narrowly. I also thank Mrs. Suzanne Mitchell, for her continued service as my editor. This book is improved by her skillful pen. Both of these choice servants are like Onesiphorus in that they have "often refreshed me" (2 Tim. 1:16).

I also thank Dr. Ron Allchin, for his kind remarks and the role that the Biblical Counseling Center is having as it assists in equipping the local church to counsel the Word; and Dr. John Street of The Master's University and Master's Seminary, for being so gracious and kind in writing the Foreword to this book.

Lastly, I am thankful for the example of faithful expositors who have greatly influenced my life and how I minister the Word of God to my flock. This includes John MacArthur and Steve Lawson, who have graciously read and endorsed this book, not to mention the many faithful men who have already gone before us but who live on through the printed page.

# CONTENTS

# FOREWORD

It is unfortunate that the idea of Christians counseling one another has largely fallen into disfavor in the contemporary church. If you were to admonish average born-again Christians and church shepherds with the responsibility of counseling others, the common excuse would often be, "I'm not a counselor! That's something for a credentialed professional with a special gift and a PhD." Counseling is not conceived as a significant aspect of personal ministry for individual Christians or pastors in the church. For them, counseling is complicated, private and messy, something reserved for the specialist. This sophisticated, often sullied job is not the type most Christians are anxious to pursue. Essentially, this attitude has greatly diminished the personal ministry of the Word of God and gravely weakened the church.

How has such a narrow and negative view of Christians counseling one another become so entrenched in the church? For many pastors, it begins in the seminary. Most pastoral counseling classes strictly train pastors so that they are ill-equipped to handle serious soul turmoil, much less teach others to do so. Theological training is insufficient to deal with refined layers of consciousness. Only a licensed psychotherapist has the educated insight to decipher the complexities of the psyche. When this occurs, a seminary has tacitly acknowledged that the Bible is at best a primitive psychology, insufficiently sophisticated in matters of the soul.

Additionally, many seminaries teach a truncated view of ministry. Pulpit preaching is the exclusive task of the pastor, not counseling. Many men go to seminary to learn how to preach sermons, not shepherd individual souls or train congregations to counsel. As long as a pastor can preach a good sermon, he is well equipped to pastor a church. But not only does this concept of pastoral ministry violate the discipleship ministry of the New Testament church (Acts 20:20, 31; Col. 1:28–29), it is also a wrong view of preaching. Preaching today is often restricted to the delivery of homiletical sermons from a church pulpit. But the New Testament semantic range of the word (2 Tim. 4:2; "to preach," Greek *kerusso*) is much broader and encompasses the meaning of the personal preaching of the Word through counseling.[1] One-on-one counseling is one form of proclaiming or preaching the Word, other than the proclamation of the Word from a pulpit.

Like their pastors, most Christians have adopted a professionalized or psychologized view of counseling that naturally excludes uneducated laity. This is why I believe this book, *Discipling the Flock*, addresses a serious deficiency in the discipleship ministry of Christians within the church. It advocates a radical departure from the status quo and a return to an authentic personal ministry of the Word among Christians through discipleship counseling. It effectively lays the theological foundation for Christians regaining the New Testament priority of addressing personal soul troubles with biblical counsel.

Dr. John D. Street
Chair, Graduate Program in Biblical Counseling, The Master's University and Seminary, Santa Clarita, California

# Chapter One:

# A SHEPHERD AFTER GOD'S OWN HEART

*Then I will give you shepherds after My own heart, who will feed you on knowledge and understanding.*

*–Jeremiah 3:15*

One of the surest signs of the blessing of God upon His people is the gift of spiritual shepherds who intentionally disciple and faithfully care for His flock. Yet this truth is virtually unknown to our present generation, whose heart has been captivated by the marriage of man-centered theology with church-growth theory and their firstborn child, pragmatic methodology. The result of this is the devolution of pastors from Word-driven shepherds who nurture and care for the souls of their people into business professionals who farm out wounded sheep to psychological counselors, falling short of meeting the real needs of real people within the church. Therefore, it is time to repent.

Since judgment shall first come to the household of God (1 Peter 4:17), that is where repentance must begin. And the church's readiness to repent will be marked by God doing as He promised to Judah: "Then I will give you shepherds after My own heart, who will feed you on knowledge and understanding" (Jer. 3:15).

## SHEPHERDS GONE ASTRAY

The book of Jeremiah is essentially a long essay on apostasy. What is of particular interest is its evidence of the incredible power of leaders to influence people for good or for ill. The prophet begins with a pathetic description of the state of spiritual leadership in Judah: "The priests did not say, 'Where is the Lord?' And those who handle the law did not know Me; the rulers also transgressed against Me, and the prophets prophesied by Baal and walked after things that did not profit" (2:8). What a tragedy! The very men who were supposed to lead the people *to* God did not even *know* God. As a result, "An appalling and horrible thing has happened in the land: the prophets prophesy falsely, and the priests rule on their own authority; and My people love it so!" (5:30–31). Leaders ruled independently of God because they had already rejected the authority of His Word: "Behold, the word of the Lord has become a reproach to them; they have no delight in it" (6:10). The more the shepherds neglected the ministry of the Word of God and did ministry their own way, being "greedy for gain" (6:13), the more they offered God's people false forms of healing. "And they have healed the brokenness of My people superficially, saying, 'Peace, peace,' but there is no peace" (6:14). And naïve sheep loved it! But God did not.

Instead, God's tender love for His flock moved Him to grieve over this neglect. And so it is today. When God's sheep are "healed" superficially with theories that do not originate in His Word, psychological "felt needs" are stroked by preaching that only affirms, and emotional problems are "treated" by therapeutic counseling, people's outward symptoms may be nursed while the core problem of the heart is often ignored. As a result, the people of God are given false hope which ultimately leads to disaster. "Hear, O earth: behold, I am bringing disaster on this people, the fruit of their plans, because they have not listened to My words" (6:19). When God's shepherds neglect His Word, the flock always suffers. There is no way around it. Unfortunately, the general state of church leadership today is not much better than it was in Jeremiah's time.

*Leadership* journal has been a prominent periodical directed toward pastors and church leaders for decades. After studying its shift away from the Word of God as well as devotion to theology, David Wells concludes,

> As the journal turns away from the Bible to what it apparently assumes are more fruitful sources of knowledge it is redefining Christian ministry and the pastor who accepts its point of view. In the study, the evangelical pastor is now the C.E.O.; in the pulpit, the pastor is a psychologist whose task it is to engineer good relations and warm feelings.[1]

Fifteen years later, in another book, *The Courage to Be Protestant*, Wells indicates that "the lay of the evangelical land" has not improved, but in fact has worsened, giving way to a new kind of leadership among pastors.

> Gone is the older model of the scholar-saint, one who was as comfortable with books and learning as with the aches of the soul. This was the shepherd who knew the flock, knew how to tend it, and Sunday by Sunday took that flock into the treasures of God's Word. This has changed. In its place is the new "celebrity" style. What we typically see now, Nancy Pearcey suggests, is the leader who works by manipulating the feelings of the audience, enhancing his own image with personal anecdotes, modeling himself after the CEO, and adopting a domineering management style. He (usually) is completely results-oriented, pragmatic, happy to employ any technique from the secular world that will produce the desired results.[2]

In other words, the very nature of the pastorate is being intentionally overhauled and the "new" worldly paradigm does not look much different from that which God condemned in the Old Testament.

So what I am calling for in this book is a new crop of teaching shepherds who are both tenacious and tender: tenacious in their study and preaching of the whole counsel of God, and tender in their application of its promises and demands to the lives of God's sheep through the personal and pastoral ministry of counseling; that is, discipleship targeted at specific areas of life where biblical change is necessary. This biblical theology of discipleship is thoroughly defended in my companion book, *Counseling One Another*,[3] which presents a complete picture of the role that every believer has in the work of making disciples of Jesus Christ. However, the focus of this smaller book is on the key part that pastors and elders have in the discipleship process, primarily by means of our role as *teaching shepherds* who lead the lambs of God toward maturity in Jesus Christ by means of the personal ministry of discipleship and the public ministry of preaching.

## SHEPHERDING IS OUR BUSINESS

Isaiah describes God this way: "Like a shepherd He will tend His flock, in His arm He will gather the lambs and carry them in His bosom; He will gently lead the nursing ewes" (Isa. 40:11). Jesus refers to Himself as the Good Shepherd who cares for His sheep by leading them, protecting them from danger, and calling them by name because He knows them (John 10:1–15). Since the word from which we get "pastor" means "shepherd,"[4] and God uses this word-picture to describe Himself, it is essential for us to consider the expectation that He places on His undershepherds to care for His flock. This is our business.

According to 1 Peter 5:2, the main function of pastor-elders is to care for the flock of God: "shepherd the flock of God among you, exercising oversight." Addressing the Ephesian elders, Paul says essentially the same thing when he exhorts them to be "on guard for yourselves and for all the flock, among which the Holy Spirit has made you *overseers*, to *shepherd* the church of God which He purchased with His own blood" (Acts 20:28).[5] Effective shepherding consists of caring for the overall spiritual well-being of God's sheep, which requires feeding them the Word of God, leading them by example into paths of righteousness for His name's sake, and protecting them from spiritual hazards.

Faithful shepherding requires feeding God's sheep the spiritual food they need in order to grow to maturity. God sharply rebuked those who did not provide nourishment to Israel but instead took care of themselves. Both Jeremiah and Ezekiel issue forth woes to lazy shepherds:

> "Woe to the shepherds who are destroying and scattering the sheep of My pasture!" declares the LORD. Therefore thus says the LORD God of Israel concerning the shepherds who are tending My people: "You have scattered My flock and driven them away, and *have not attended to them*; behold, I am about to attend to you for the evil of your deeds," declares the LORD.
>
> Jer. 23:1–2

> Son of man, prophesy against the shepherds of Israel. Prophesy and say to those shepherds, "Thus says the Lord GOD, 'Woe, shepherds of Israel who have been feeding themselves! *Should not the shepherds feed the flock?* You eat the fat and clothe yourselves with the wool, you slaughter the fat sheep *without feeding* the flock.'"
>
> Ezek. 34:2–3

Clearly, God's expectation is that we attend to His sheep. To do so, we must heed Solomon's counsel to "Know well the condition of [our] flocks, and pay attention to [our] herds" (Prov. 27:23). If we as shepherds do not know our sheep, how can we properly care for them? And how can we care for them without feeding them? And how will they become fruit bearing disciples if we do not feed them?

The most essential ingredient in the diet that we must feed believers is sound doctrine that will nourish their souls (1 Tim. 4:6). This satisfies the young believer's longing for "the pure milk of the word," so that he or she may grow in respect to salvation (1 Peter 2:2), as well as the mature believer's hunger for "solid food" to grow in discernment (Heb. 5:12–14). This is undoubtedly why Jesus commanded Peter three times to *feed* His sheep (John 21:15–17).

By feeding God's sheep the pure truth of Scripture, faithful shepherds also lead them into paths of righteousness. If we do not do this consistently, the people of God will be led astray. Jeremiah declares, "For the shepherds have become stupid and have not sought the Lord, therefore they have not prospered, and all their flock is scattered" (Jer. 10:21). Jesus models faithful leadership when, as the Good Shepherd, He calls believers by name and safely leads us to pasture (John 10:3–11). Applying this to the local church, it is right to conclude that a good pastor leads his flock to God. He is not there simply to marry and bury, but he works in cooperation with the Holy Spirit to lead God's sheep onto the path of truth, taking them to depths of maturity and heights of ministry as he himself also walks the walk of faith.

This kind of leadership requires that we continually protect God's flock. One reason why Paul instructed the Ephesian elders to guard the flock is because believers are constantly being preyed upon by savage wolves. They need protection against false teachers who emerge from within the church and tear her apart, "not sparing the flock" (Acts 20:28–29). Peter also warns,

> . . . there will . . . be false teachers among you, who will secretly introduce destructive heresies, even denying the Master who bought them, bringing swift destruction upon themselves. Many will follow their sensuality, and because of them the way of the truth will be maligned; and in their greed they will exploit you with false words; their judgment from long ago is not idle, and their destruction is not asleep.
>
> 2 Peter 2:1–3

Tragically, many believers throughout biblical history were led astray by unfaithful shepherds. "My people have become lost sheep; their shepherds have led them astray" (Jer. 50:6). J. C. Ryle argues that the most effective protection against this grave danger is for believers to know the Word of God:

> What is the best safe-guard against false teaching? Beyond all doubt the regular study of the word of God, with prayer for the teaching of the Holy Spirit. The Bible was given to be a lamp to our feet and a light to our path (Psalm 119:105). The man who reads it aright will never be allowed greatly to err. It is neglect of the Bible which makes so many a prey to the first false teacher whom they hear. They would have us believe that "they are not learned, and do not pretend to have decided opinions." The plain truth is that they are lazy and idle about reading the Bible, and do not like the trouble of thinking for themselves. Nothing supplies false prophets with followers so much as spiritual sloth under a cloak of humility. May we all bear in mind our Lord's warning! The world, the devil, and the flesh, are not the only dangers in the way of the Christian. There remains another yet, and that is the "false prophet," the wolf "in sheep's clothing." Happy is he who prays over his Bible and knows the difference between truth and error in religion! There is a difference, and we are meant to know it, and use our knowledge.[6]

Therefore, church shepherds must protect the people of God through the persistent teaching of biblical truth so that believers discipline their lives and their thinking processes to be in subjection to the Word, which will produce the fruit of spiritual discernment. This is why God requires that elders be "able to teach," and be men who hold to the truth so that they are "able both to exhort in sound doctrine and to refute those who contradict" (1 Tim. 3:2; 2 Tim. 2:2, 24; Titus 1:9). God not only equips us for this calling by the Spirit, but He also exhorts us to be diligent in study so that we may be approved by God as workmen who do not need to be ashamed (2 Tim. 2:15). For that reason, faithful shepherds must view themselves as lifelong students, understanding, as Charles Spurgeon did, that "He who has ceased to learn has ceased to teach. He who no longer sows in the study will no more reap in the pulpit."[7] We must "kindle afresh the gift of God" within us (2 Tim. 1:6). This is what it means to be a shepherd after God's own heart.

If and when the church repents of her love affair with man-centered theology, psychological theory, and worldly methodology, God will once again give His people teaching shepherds who will feed them on biblical knowledge, help them understand it, and patiently lead them to apply it to lives characterized by progressive godliness. The evidence of this will be disciples who display growing love for Jesus, the living Word, and growing obedience to the Bible, the written Word of God. If repentance must begin with the household of God, then, even more so, repentance must take place in the pastor's study, the counseling room, and the pulpit. My fellow minister, that is what this book is all about.

## THE PURPOSE OF THIS BOOK

In short, the purpose of this book is to call pastors and elders back to authentic biblical discipleship—back to the immeasurable privilege and indispensable task of shepherding the flock of God by means of teaching the Word of God and caring for the souls of men and women. This purpose will be accomplished by delving into the Apostle Paul's philosophy of ministry as it pertains to the relationship of counseling to preaching, and preaching to counseling—both being essential parts of the shepherding task. The exposition of two key New Testament passages revealing this apostolic commitment forms the heart of this book.

Chapter 2 unveils the portrait of an authentic disciple-making minister that is painted by Paul in Colossians 1:24–29. Chapter 3 clarifies the key role of the pastor in the discipleship process as the gifted teacher and equipper of God's saints described in Ephesians 4:11–16. Finally, Chapter 4 reviews God's call to church shepherds and unwraps the eternal reward that will be given to those who are faithful. Without a doubt, ministers have a stewardship from God, a privileged responsibility to function as undershepherds for Christ, the Chief Shepherd, before whom we will one day give an account (1 Peter 5:4).

# Chapter Two:

# A Shepherd Leads God's Flock to Spiritual Maturity

*We proclaim Him, admonishing every man and teaching every man with all wisdom, so that we may present every man complete in Christ. For this purpose also I labor, striving according to His power, which mightily works within me.*

*–Colossians 1:28–29*

Authentic biblical shepherding requires a personal commitment to do all that is superhumanly possible to help fellow believers grow to maturity in Jesus Christ. This is accomplished by means of instruction and correction according to His power, which mightily works within the shepherd and his sheep by the Holy Spirit sent from God. God's vision of discipleship, therefore, requires that we recognize this process as a stewardship from Him entailing intensive labor on behalf of others within the mutual experience of suffering in a sin-sick world. Consequently, we must be committed to Christ-centered ministry that continually builds believers on the solid foundation of His wisdom—God's truth applied to life. To accomplish this, we must depend on the life-changing power of the Holy Spirit as we struggle toward the goal of being conformed ourselves, and conforming others, to the image of Jesus Christ.

Besides the example of Jesus, there is no greater biblical illustration of commitment to selfless ministry on behalf of others than that of the Apostle Paul.

> Now I rejoice in my sufferings for your sake, and in my flesh I do my share on behalf of His body, which is the church, in filling up what is lacking in Christ's afflictions. Of this church I was made a minister according to the stewardship from God bestowed on me for your benefit, so that I might fully carry out the preaching of the word of God, that is, the mystery which has been hidden from the past ages and generations; but has now been manifested to His saints, to whom God willed to make known what is the riches of the glory of this mystery among the Gentiles, which is Christ in you, the hope of glory. We proclaim Him, admonishing every man and teaching every man with all wisdom, so that we may present every man complete in Christ. For this purpose also I labor, striving according to His power, which mightily works within me.
>
> Col. 1:24–29

This passage reveals four elements of the kind of ministry that serves as a model for personal discipleship counseling that will lead others toward the spiritual maturity that should characterize believers in Jesus Christ.

## THE PRICE OF AUTHENTIC MINISTRY

The first element is the price that we must be willing to pay to be ministers of God. "Now I rejoice in my sufferings for your sake, and in my flesh I do my share on behalf of His body, which is the church, in filling up what is lacking in Christ's afflictions" (v. 24). Paul believed that the price of authentic ministry is a willingness to endure suffering on behalf of others. This requires attachment to people. It demands that pastors and elders be involved in others' lives far beyond preaching and teaching to them each Sunday. It discourages us from keeping a distance from our people, especially from those we may consider to be "needy" disciples who require a large investment of time and energy. In *Rediscovering Pastoral Ministry*, Lance Quinn makes a case for this to his fellow ministers:

> Our role as pastors also demands that we be disciple-makers. We cannot be pulpiteers who preach at our people but have no involvement in their lives. The process only begins with the proclamation of Scripture. It finds its real fruition across the entire spectrum of the shepherd's work—feeding, leading, cleaning, bandaging, protecting, nurturing, and every other aspect of a tender shepherd's loving care. This is the process of discipling.[1]

This vital connection to the lives of people is often birthed out of the common grounds of pain and suffering. In Paul's case, he was writing from a prison in Rome. Epaphras had traveled there to visit him and to report on the progress of the believers in Asia Minor. No doubt Paul was encouraged to learn of the Colossians' "love in the Spirit" (1:8), but he was also concerned to hear how the heresies of Gnosticism were drawing these Christians away from the reality of the fullness of their new life in Christ (2:1–3). Therefore, he wrote his letter and sent it to them by his "fellow bond-servant in the Lord," Tychicus (4:7). But in spite of "the daily pressure on [him] of concern for all the churches" (of which he testified in 2 Cor. 11:28), Paul rejoiced in his suffering because he knew that it stimulated growth in others.

The point must also be made that Paul's suffering was not merely physical, but emotional as well. Pain traveled with him wherever he went. The cause of this "pressure" was his intense love for the people God had called him to serve and his undying commitment to do everything in his power to help them become like Jesus. Suffering, consequently, empowers ministry in at least three ways.

## SUFFERING LEADS TO DEEPER, MORE LASTING GROWTH

First, Paul chose to find joy in the midst of suffering because he knew it would benefit those to whom he ministered. He was committed to doing his "share on behalf of [Christ's] body" (Col. 1:24) in spite of personal trial. Robert Gromacki comments, "Christ suffered in death to save the church, and now Paul suffered in life to spare it."[2] Paul understood that real-life ministry to real-life sinners was not an easy career choice. It would require his very life. It was God's appointment for him. Immediately following Paul's conversion, Jesus revealed this to Ananias of Damascus: "Go, for he is a chosen instrument of Mine, to bear My name before the Gentiles and kings and the sons of Israel; *for I will show him how much he must suffer* for My name's sake" (Acts 9:15–16).

Paul's willingness to suffer for the sake of the church sprang from his desire to fill up "what is lacking in Christ's afflictions." The word "lacking" does not mean the sufferings of Christ are insufficient for salvation, but rather that there is much more suffering that needs to take place so that the ends of the earth can see Christ's love, grace, and mercy illustrated by living witnesses. John Piper explains,

> Christ's afflictions are not lacking in their atoning sufficiency. They are lacking in that they are not known and felt by people who were not at the cross. Paul dedicates himself not only to carry the message of those sufferings to the nations, but also to suffer with Christ and for Christ in such a way that what people see are "Christ's sufferings." In this way he follows the pattern of Christ by laying down his life for the life of the church. "I endure everything for the sake of the elect that they may obtain salvation in Christ Jesus with its eternal glory" (2 Tim. 2:10).[3]

As servants of Christ suffer for His name, and for the sake of His righteousness, the message of the cross continues to be proclaimed. This was also true in Philippi, where God used Paul's imprisonment to bring about "the greater progress of the gospel" (Phil. 1:12), which specifically resulted in the message of Christ being made known to "the whole praetorian guard" (1:13).

A more recent illustration is told by Alex Leonovich, Executive Secretary of Slavic Missionary Service. After emigrating from Russia to the United States with his parents and younger brother in 1929, Alex received missionary training at Nyack College in New York. As a result, his heart became burdened to reach the Soviet Union with the gospel, which resulted in his direction of the Russian Gospel Broadcasts from HCJB in Quito, Ecuador. Later, the demise of the Soviet Union allowed him to revisit his homeland. After decades of faithful broadcasting, and unaware of who had been listening across the ocean, Alex arrived to be greeted by standing-room-only crowds of believers whose faith had been fed via his radio teaching. On one of his return visits, at the time of a historic prayer meeting in the Lubyanka (KGB headquarters), Alex met a believer named Basil Paley. Alex tells the story of their meeting:

> When we opened the door … who should stand there but a broad-shouldered man with disheveled hair all over his face, two missing front teeth and a look of bewilderment on his face. After looking at the whole group, he spotted me and, almost like a locomotive, came charging at me and kissed me eighteen times on my cheek, saying in a bullhorn voice, "Brother Alex, this is for every year that I spent in prison for my faith." I looked at him in amazement. In shock, really. I had never seen him before. I knew nothing about him. I'd never met him. Then, through tears, he told me his story: "Yours was the last face that I saw; the last message that I heard before I was exiled to Siberia. In the 1960s, I was living in Ukraine where I was sought by the government for printing gospel literature on a little press I had made out of washing machine parts. I distributed 700,000 little leaflets and gospels house to house in different areas during the darkness of night so I wouldn't be seen or heard. I had been in prison before and would have been arrested again if I had attended church, so I did my growing by listening to your radio broadcast. When I heard you were going to be in Kiev in 1965, I wanted to hear you in person so much that I decided to risk coming to hear you. As you know,

every service was monitored by the KGB and everything was carefully scrutinized. Even though I was far from my home, the secret police recognized me, arrested me as I left the service and took me to prison. From there, I was exiled to Vorkuta where I spent eighteen years at hard labor. Yours was the last face I saw and yours was the last message I heard from the pulpit before I was sent to Siberia. You preached about Christ asking Peter the question, 'Lovest thou Me?' Every time it got so unbearably hard and difficult in prison that I felt almost forgotten not only by man but even by God, I would see your face and hear you speaking that question. It was as if Christ was asking Peter—and me—'Lovest thou Me?' Then I would lift my head toward heaven and say, 'Lord, you know all things; You know that I love you.' For a while, I couldn't figure out why God would allow me to be punished for serving Him. Then, one morning, I saw that God had provided a new way to serve Him. Each day, we had to line up long before the sun came up. Prisoners had to be prompt, but guards did not. That meant that thousands of us stood outdoors with nothing to do. I decided to use those minutes to preach. I asked the guards for permission and they said I could if I would agree to do the filthiest job—clean the toilets." Basil spoke with such force and animation that I grabbed his flailing arms several times as I pleaded with him to speak softer and slower so I could translate what he was saying into English. It was to no avail. He would lower his head and try to speak slower and more quietly, but within seconds, he would again be shouting like a machine gun. I soon learned why. "In the beginning, I became hoarse as I tried to be heard by all the thousands of prisoners standing in line. Then, gradually, my voice became stronger. I never knew if I would have even two minutes in which to preach, so I learned to speak at top speeds and loud volumes. Sometimes it took two weeks to complete one sermon. But I've been back, and

> there's still a community of about 100 believers worshiping in that camp," Basil told us, bathing us in the warmth of his enormous crooked smile.[4]

God's servants may be bound in locks and chains, and punished for their bold preaching, but the power of His gospel cannot be shackled. Men may be imprisoned; words cannot be.

Experiences similar to this led the Apostle Paul to confidently exhort Timothy, "Remember Jesus Christ, risen from the dead, descendant of David, according to my gospel, *for which I suffer hardship* even to imprisonment as a criminal; but the word of God is not imprisoned" (2 Tim. 2:8–9). Jesus told His disciples, "Remember the word that I said to you, 'A slave is not greater than his master.' If they persecuted Me, they will also persecute you" (John 15:20). The afflictions Paul suffered were intense because He suffered in his master's place and he knew that his suffering was profitable for the churches because the courage he received from the Lord drew not only him but also them closer to Christ. It was the price he had to pay for their growth. He was not a half-hearted, apathetic, do-as-little-as-I-can-to-get-by minister of the gospel. Nothing short of total life commitment to total life change in his disciples would do! Such is the commitment of any authentic minister of the gospel.

Richard Baxter, a Puritan minister in the 1600s, is most readily recognized as the author of *The Reformed Pastor*. This publication was not entitled "reformed" for doctrinal reasons, but rather because it called for a *reformation* among his fellow ministers of the gospel. It was corrective counsel in book form. Since its original appearance in 1656, *The Reformed Pastor* has been a sober call to ministers to be serious about the gospel and their own personal holiness. In his Preface written in 1829, William Brown states, "Hard must be the heart of that minister, who can read it without being moved, melted, and overwhelmed, under a sense of his own shortcomings; hard must be his heart, if he be not roused to greater faithfulness, diligence, and activity in winning souls to Christ."[5] In the book, Baxter also appeals to his fellow pastors to suffer *with* their flock: "If you are ministers of Christ indeed, you will long for the perfecting of his body, and the gathering in of his elect; and you will 'travail as in birth' until Christ be formed in the souls of your people."[6] Serving Christ includes suffering, but suffering produces lasting growth as God uses it to substantiate our ministry and spread the gospel to people who would not otherwise have been touched by our lives.

### Suffering helps us comfort others

Second, Paul rejoiced in his sufferings because he knew that God was using them to produce growth in his own life through the experience of receiving divine comfort, which would then touch the lives of those whom he served.[7] Writing to the Corinthians, he says, "Blessed be the God and Father of our Lord Jesus Christ, the Father of mercies and God of all comfort, who comforts us in all our affliction *so that we will be able to comfort those who are in any affliction* with the comfort with which we ourselves are comforted by God" (2 Cor. 1:3–4). Suffering enhances ministry because it produces a common ground on which to relate to others who are in the midst of the same types of trials that we have already experienced and endured.

I can add personal testimony to this benefit. Four of our ten children are profoundly hearing-impaired, one totally deaf at birth. I have come to believe that one of the many reasons why God gave us these children is so that the believers in our local church can witness God's power being made perfect in our weakness (2 Cor. 12:9). Too many Christians have the strange idea that pastors and their families do not have the same struggles that they have, but those believers are wrong. The pressure of hearing-impairment, numerous cochlear implant surgeries, and ongoing speech, language, and physical therapy in our children's lives takes us to a deeper level of dependence on God, which in turn gives our church something it would not otherwise have—an environment in which people are free to endure with one another instead of trying to battle adversity alone. When their minister suffers with them, they are free to grow.

There is no power in our strength, but there is much power in our weakness—God's power—made infinitely more visible and glorious against the backdrop of our frail humanity. I am convinced that the more trials we endure as shepherds, the more opportunities God will give us to comfort those who will have to walk where we have limped so that we may dispense the same grace that we received along the way. Jerry Bridges, in his outstanding book *Trusting God*, offers this insight into the value of suffering:

> We can be sure that the development of Christlike character will not occur in our lives without adversity … [God] will not remove the adversity until we have profited from it and developed in whatever way He intended in bringing or allowing it into our lives … God does not delight in our sufferings. He brings only that which is necessary, but He does not shrink from that which will help us grow.[8]

God is the potter and we are the clay. He will use the pain of suffering to mold us, to remove or smooth out hardened lumps, so that we will be more useful ministers of God's comfort.

### SUFFERING KEEPS US FROM EXALTING OURSELVES

Third, suffering enhances ministry because of its unique ability to slay our pride. Paul confesses this in 2 Corinthians 12:7–10:

> Because of the surpassing greatness of the revelations, for this reason, to keep me from exalting myself, there was given me a thorn in the flesh, a messenger of Satan to torment me—to keep me from exalting myself! Concerning this I implored the Lord three times that it might leave me. And He has said to me, "My grace is sufficient for you, for power is perfected in weakness." Most gladly, therefore, I will rather boast about my weaknesses, so that the power of Christ may dwell in me. Therefore I am well content with weaknesses, with insults, with distresses, with persecutions,

> with difficulties, for Christ's sake; for when I am weak, then I am strong.

God custom-designed suffering for Paul's benefit because He knew that the magnitude of his heavenly experience could easily cause pride to well up in the apostle's heart, which would render him less useful in the Lord's work. His suffering was not merely allowed by God—it was *appointed* by Him. This planned appointment with pain brought more glory to God by taking attention away from Paul's natural abilities. In fact, adversity is one of the favored methods God uses to purify us for greater ministry, as Charles Spurgeon recognizes:

> Our God takes care always to have security that, if he works a great work by us, we shall not appropriate the glory of it to ourselves. He brings us down lower and lower in our own esteem … Some trumpets are so stuffed with self that God cannot blow through them. You may rest quite certain that, if God honours a man in public, he takes him aside privately, and flogs him well, otherwise he would get elevated and proud, and God will not have that.[9]

The price of ministry is suffering. This pain, whether external or internal, is not a hindrance to our service for Christ. Instead, it enhances it by leading to deeper growth in us and in our churches, teaching us how to comfort others with the grace of experience, and weakening the base of pride so that we will be more useful to the God who is "opposed to the proud, but gives grace to the humble" (James 4:6).

## THE PERSONALITY OF AUTHENTIC MINISTRY

Returning to our passage in Colossians, the second element of an authentic discipleship ministry is its "personality," which includes seven characteristics that describe Paul's ministry of the Word of God.

### Responsible shepherding

First, we see that Paul had been made a minister of the church "according to the stewardship from God" (1:25*a*). "Stewardship" indicates "the responsibility, authority, and obligation given to a household slave."[10] In other words, Paul had been called to a place of responsibility in God's house and was, therefore, concerned about completing his work.

As an undershepherd of God's flock, he ministered with the constant awareness that one day he would give an account to the Chief Shepherd, and it was He whom Paul wanted to please the most (2 Tim. 4:1; 1 Peter 5:4). Yet, like most of us, he also battled the fear of man. "The fear of man brings a snare," a trap that enslaves us to the opinions and approval of men, "but he who trusts in the LORD will be exalted" (Prov. 29:25). However, the Spirit helped Paul to make some progress in his own growth so that when it came time to write to the Galatians, he was able to testify, "If I were *still* trying to please men, I would not be a bond-servant of Christ" (Gal. 1:10).

The authentic servant of God understands that he can be a God-pleaser *or* a man-pleaser, but not both. Unfaithfulness to God's calling equals unfaithfulness to God. Therefore, he approaches every aspect of his calling responsibly. This requires him to discipline himself to remember that the success of his ministry will not be measured during his own lifetime. Rather, it will be at the Judgment Seat of Christ that "the quality of each man's work" will become evident (1 Cor. 3:13). To remind myself of this, I have taped to my computer screen this quote from Warren Wiersbe: "Keep in mind that the harvest is not the end of the meeting: it is the end of the age."[11]

First Corinthians 4:1–2 reminds us that faithfulness will be the basis upon which God judges His stewards. "Let a man so consider us, as servants of Christ and stewards of the mysteries of God. Moreover it is required in stewards that one be found faithful" (NKJV). Authentic ministry, therefore, is responsible ministry. If we are not engaged in helping disciples grow in and through their personal problems, then we are not being faithful as stewards of the Great Command (Matt. 28:19–20), which is to produce followers of Jesus whose lives characterize the walk of faith and obedience to His Word.[12]

### Servant-like shepherding

The second aspect of the personality of authentic ministry is its servanthood. This is made plain in the phrase "for your benefit" (Col. 1:25). God made Paul a steward of the church not for the apostle's personal gain, but for the spiritual prosperity of others. Paul was clearly saying, "My ministry is for *you*, not for me." And in doing so, he was following his Master, who washed the filthy feet of His argumentative disciples and then said to them, "For I gave you an example that you also should do as I did to you" (John 13:15). Picking up the pitcher and towel was an object lesson on being a servant and symbolized Jesus' calling. "For even the Son of Man did not come to be served, but to serve, and to give His life a ransom for many" (Mark 10:45).

When defending his apostolic ministry before the false accusers in Corinth, Paul made it abundantly clear that the ministry of the gospel is a matter of sincere service to God rather than personal profit. As a servant, he was "a fragrance of Christ to God among those who are being saved and among those who are perishing … For we are not like many, peddling the word of God, but as from sincerity, but as from God, we speak in Christ in the sight of God" (2 Cor. 2:15–17). Authentic biblical ministry exists for the sake of others rather than for the profit of the minister.

### Word-saturated shepherding

Third, the personality of authentic ministry includes its confidence in the power of the Holy Spirit through the written Word to accomplish the work of sanctification. There is no question that Paul thoroughly believed that the heart of his stewardship was the Word of God itself. God bestowed responsibility on him that he "might fully carry out the preaching of the word of God" (Col. 1:25*b*). The chief substance of his preaching was "the mystery which has been hidden from the past ages and generations" (v. 26). In the New Testament, "mystery" refers to something that was unknowable by common human means. In other words, it required divine revelation. Specifically, in Colossians 1:27, the once-hidden truth now revealed is "Christ in you, the hope of glory."

The indwelling Christ living His life in and through the life of the believer is a mystery, something previously unknown by millennia of believers. This biblical truth saturates the preaching and discipleship writings of Paul. Because "Christ is in you," he writes to the believers in Rome, "the body is dead because of sin, yet the spirit is alive because of righteousness" (Rom. 8:10). He urges the Corinthians who are losing the battle against sin, "Test yourselves to see if you are in the faith; examine yourselves! Or do you not recognize this about yourselves, that *Jesus Christ is in you*—unless indeed you fail the test?" (2 Cor. 13:5). Paul's own testimony of how to live the Christian life is clearly stated: "I have been crucified with Christ; and it is no longer I who live, but *Christ lives in me*" (Gal. 2:20). This is our "hope of glory," the hope we have of one day being glorified in the presence of our Savior, free from this body of sin and death, held safe by the life of Christ within us by means of the sealing work of the Spirit of God (1 John 3:2; Rom. 7:24–25; Eph. 1:13).

As authentic shepherds, therefore, we must keep the Word of God central in discipleship. The written Word is fundamental to effective ministry because it is the instrument by which the Spirit gives birth to saving faith (Rom. 10:17) and causes us to behold the glory of Christ, thereby transforming us by the renewing of our minds (2 Cor. 3:18; Rom. 12:1–2). It is the tool by which He makes us "adequate, equipped for every good work" (2 Tim. 3:17). As ministers of the gospel, we must cling to the same promise that fortified the ministry of Isaiah:

> "For My thoughts are not your thoughts
>   Nor are your ways My ways," declares the Lord.
> "For as the heavens are higher than the earth
>   So are My ways higher than your ways
>   And My thoughts than your thoughts.
> For as the rain and the snow come down from heaven,
>   And do not return there without watering the earth
>   And making it bear and sprout,
>   And furnishing seed to the sower and bread to the
>     eater;
> So will My word be which goes forth from My mouth;

> It will not return to Me empty,
> Without accomplishing what I desire,
> And without succeeding in the matter for which I
> sent it."
>
> Isa. 55:8–11

The ministry of a Word-saturated pulpit is foundational to an effective personal-discipleship ministry. It is crucial that a faithful pulpit ministry not be undermined by the use of psychological theory in the "counseling room." As ministers loyally dispense the Word, both in public and in private, believers will grow in the comprehension of their sufficiency in Christ. In other words, every formal "counseling session," "discipleship small group," informal "encouragement-over-coffee," or gentle "breakfast confrontation" must be used as an opportunity to wisely bestow God's words to the person's particular need. We have no other power. We have no other instrument with which to perform heart surgery (Heb. 4:12). Our help must be Word-saturated or it is not authentic biblical shepherding.

### CHRIST-CENTERED SHEPHERDING

Fourth, Paul's intentional strategy was to preach the person and work of Jesus Christ: "And we proclaim Him" (Col. 1:28*a*). "Proclaim" is in the present tense in the Greek, meaning it was a continual action for him. In other words, it was his habit to announce Christ as the solution to every sin struggle. Paul always used the written Word of God to draw the attention back to the living Word—Jesus Christ. His dedication to Christ-centered shepherding grew out of his desire that "their hearts may be encouraged, having been knit together in love, and attaining to all the wealth that comes from the full assurance of understanding, resulting in a true knowledge of God's mystery, that is, *Christ Himself*, in whom are hidden all the treasures of wisdom and knowledge" (2:2–3). Knowledge that is not Christ-centered is knowledge not worth knowing.

What prompted Paul to make this point in the book of Colossians was the Gnosticism that threatened to diminish the work of Christ and

His preeminence. In the *International Standard Bible Encyclopedia*, John Rutherford says, "The intellectual pride of the Gnostics refined away the Gospel into a philosophy."[13] This philosophy then ensnared people because it appealed "to the higher intellectual tastes."[14] In Colossae, as in Corinth, intellectualism threatened to replace biblical faith (1 Cor. 1:20–25).

In his day, Martyn Lloyd-Jones observed this same trend in evangelicalism and warned, "Philosophy has always been the cause of the church going astray, for philosophy means, ultimately, a trusting to human reason and human understanding."[15] When this happens, Christians are deceived through distraction, by their focus being shifted from the person of Christ, not only as the source of their salvation, but also as the means of their sanctification.

In contrast to philosophy, the Bible clearly presents the answer to our sin problem not as an idea, but as a person—Jesus Christ, God in the flesh having come to rescue us from our sin. David Powlison explains this well:

> Truth mediates a Person, a working Redeemer. To be human is to love a Savior, Father, Master, and Lord. Instead of "psychopathology" and "syndromes," we see "sins" against this Person, and we see sufferings that are "trials" revealing our need for a true Deliverer and refuge. Instead of proposing that some psychodynamic insight, met need, altered self-talk, or behavioral rehabituation will cure us, we receive God's actual mercies as our salvation. Instead of defining change as an intra-psychic, psychosocial, or biological process of "healing" or "growth," we define change as turning to a Person whom we trust, fear, obey, and seek to please.[16]

Jesus Christ is God's solution to our need for both salvation and sanctification. It is through obedient faith in Him as our Redeemer that we are saved from the eternal punishment of sin. However, it is also through the walk of obedient faith in Him as our Master that we are progressively set apart to a life of holiness, being remade into His image as we "put on the new self, which in the likeness of God has been created in righteousness and holiness of the truth" (Eph. 4:24).

Not only had Gnosticism corrupted the doctrine of Christ in Colossae, but it also confused the believers' theology of sanctification by redirecting the focus of man's problem from the heart to the body, which Gnostics considered evil. Alexander Maclaren comments, "For if matter be the source of all evil, then the fountain of each man's sin is to be found, not in his own perverted will, but in his body, and the cure of it is to be reached, not by faith which plants a new life in a sinful spirit, but simply by ascetic mortification of the flesh."[17] As a result, sanctification in the Colossian church became merely an issue of external conformity to rules and the suppression of one's bodily cravings by sheer willpower (Col. 2:16–19).

Authentic biblical shepherding, therefore, must persistently lead others back to the Christ of the cross and the empty tomb in order to announce Him as the solution to any and every sin struggle we battle, and as the One who is worthy of our submissive obedience. There is a sense in which the field of counseling is being "Gnosticized." We live in a society in which we are continually bombarded with the idea that the problem is not internal corruption. After all, "We are all basically good people. It's just that our bodies don't work right anymore." As a result, there is often a chemical reason to explain away any and all wrong behavior, regardless of how evil it may be. And, consequently, there is a chemical savior, or pill, for every problem. As well-meaning, sincere, psychologized counselors turn man's attention away from the real problem of reigning sin in the human heart, the Savior that came to deliver us from that same sin is hidden behind a cloak of supposed biological solutions. Therefore, as biblical disciple-makers, we must be committed to Christ-centered ministry. We must relentlessly point others to Him!

## CORRECTIVE SHEPHERDING

Fifth, the model of authentic ministry displayed by the Apostle Paul includes warning disciples of the danger of false ideas and confronting sinful attitudes and actions. The word "admonishing" (Col. 1:28) comes from *noutheteo*, meaning, "to correct through instruction and warning."[18] Undoubtedly this was part of Paul's public ministry of preaching, but it went beyond that to include private exhortation and counsel. For example, in his emotional goodbye to the elders in Ephesus he reminded them that, during his three-year ministry among them, he "did not cease to admonish *each one* with tears" (Acts 20:31). Paul's counseling was not harsh or cruel, but passionate and strong when necessary. Even then, it grew from a heart full of compassion. He wept for them.

The same was true when he penned his strong admonition to the Corinthian church. He wrote, "I do not write these things to shame you, but to admonish [*noutheteo*] you as my beloved children" (1 Cor. 4:14). Paul did not rebuke them sarcastically, which would disgrace them unnecessarily, but gently, in order to correct them—to shock them by exposing their sinful behavior. He did this in order to compel them to turn away from their worldliness so that they might not be destroyed. As their spiritual father, Paul pleaded with them to submit themselves to the Word of God and, therefore, to the process of biblical change.

When Paul wrote to the Thessalonian church, he was calling all believers to a ministry of corrective love, which he faithfully modeled as a minister of God. A key verse to consider regarding this one-another ministry is found in Paul's first letter to the Thessalonians: "We urge you, brethren, admonish the unruly, encourage the fainthearted, help the weak, be patient with everyone" (1 Thes. 5:14). Here we notice that every church contains at least three kinds of people who need nouthetic counseling: the unruly, the fainthearted, and the weak.

The *unruly* are those who live undisciplined, disorderly lives. "The word was primarily a military term used of the soldier who is out of step or out of rank or the army moving in disarray. It then was used more generally of whatever is out of order."[19] The undisciplined lives of some in Thessalonica were primarily characterized by willful unemployment, "doing no work at all" (2 Thes. 3:11). According to Paul, this kind of person needs to be firmly corrected and instructed concerning God's expectation of him or her as a diligent worker. Sometimes, when this person's disorderliness spills over into the church, causing dissension, even stronger action will need to be taken, as found in the apostle's letter to Titus: "Reject a factious man after a first and second warning, knowing that such a man is perverted and is sinning, being self-condemned" (3:10–11). Though all unruly behavior warrants confrontation, this is an example of destructive influence that threatens the unity of the church to the degree that it is necessary to quickly move to an advanced stage of church discipline.

The *fainthearted* need encouragement. The Greek word used here means "small-souled" or "despondent."[20] These kind of worrisome strugglers don't need firm rebuke like the unruly, but invigorating words that redirect their discouraged hearts to trust in the goodness and faithfulness of God. Jesus used words like this to help His disciples fight anxiety: "But if God so clothes the grass in the field, which is alive today and tomorrow is thrown into the furnace, how much more will He clothe you? You men of little faith!" (Luke 12:28). Therefore, our words must dispense encouragement to those in need of it.

The *weak* simply need our help. This word "probably refers to those who are morally or spiritually weak."[21] Richard Baxter writes of them,

> It is a very sad thing for Christians to be weak: it exposeth us to dangers; it abateth our consolations and delight in God, and taketh off the sweetness of wisdom's ways; it maketh us less serviceable to God and man, to bring less honour to our Master, and to do less good to all about us. We get small benefit in the use of the means of grace. We too easily play with the serpent's baits, and are ensnared by his wiles. A seducer will easily shake us, and evil may be made to appear to us as good, truth as falsehood, sin as duty … We are dishonourable to the gospel by our very weakness, and little useful to any about us.[22]

Weak believers don't need admonishment or encouragement, but they do need *help*; that is, they need to "be firmly held."[23] They need "support" (KJV) or someone to "uphold" (NKJV) them. Jesus uses this word to describe the commitment that some make to material possessions: "he will *hold to* the one and despise the other" (Matt. 6:24, KJV). Commitment, or steadfastness, is what Paul has in mind as well when he requires church overseers to be "*holding fast* the faithful word" (Titus 1:9). Our churches will include morally and spiritually weak people who need us to not let them go but instead support them and "hold their feet to the fire," in the sense of helping them grow in commitment. These brethren don't need the kind of help that feeds their weakness; they need accountability. They need to learn how to be "steadfast, immovable, always abounding in the work of the Lord" (1 Cor. 15:58).

In addition to these three kinds of believers, "everyone" needs us to have the grace of patience. "Patient" comes from a compound word meaning "long-tempered." Richard Trench argues that the noun form refers specifically to "patience with respect to persons" and cites David's long-suffering in the face of mistreatment as an example (2 Sam. 16:10–13).[24] While Shimei ran along the hillside cursing David and throwing stones at him, the king bore it patiently. This kind of long-suffering is one of the many qualities of biblical love (1 Cor. 13:4). In other words, when the biblical shepherd has a patient spirit in bearing the offenses and injuries of others, he is modeling Christlike love to those he is discipling. Richard Baxter challenges us to carry out a personal counseling ministry for the spiritual well-being of those church members who may mistreat us:

> We have to deal with distracted men who will fly in the face of their physician, but we must not, therefore, neglect their cure. He is unworthy to be a physician, who will be driven away from a phrenetic patient by foul words. Yet, alas, when sinners reproach and slander us for our love, and are more ready to spit in our faces, than to thank us for our advice, what heart-risings will there be, and how will the remnants of old Adam (pride and passion) struggle against the meekness and patience of the new man![25]

It is significant that all four of the verbs in Paul's exhortation concerning this counseling ministry—"admonish," "encourage," "help," and "be patient"—are in the present tense in the Greek, implying that these kinds of people will always be in all of our churches.

Authentic shepherding, therefore, recognizes the variety of struggles and levels of maturity within God's family and ministers with great patience, consideration, and instruction, accompanied by sensitivity from the Holy Spirit. There will never be a time before Jesus returns for His church when this kind of personal care and corrective discipleship will not be needed.

## Theological shepherding

Sixth, the personality of Paul's model for ministry includes the high priority that he places on teaching doctrine so that disciples learn to think theologically. This, of course, is an echo of the indoctrinating aspect of Jesus' command to make disciples by "*teaching* them to observe all that [He] commanded" (Matt. 28:20). "Teaching" comes from *didasko*, meaning "to give instruction."[26] The noun form simply means "doctrine."[27]

Acts 2:42 indicates that doctrine was a high priority in the early church. These believers were "continually devoting themselves to … teaching," that is, doctrine. They were being instructed in God's Word to the extent that their lives began to model truth to a dying world. First Thessalonians shows that the believers there had responded to the gospel with such eagerness and applied its theology to their lives so consistently that Paul was able to say, "You also became imitators of us and of the Lord, having received the word in much tribulation with the joy of the Holy Spirit, so that you became an example to all the believers in Macedonia and in Achaia" (1:6–7).

Sadly, evangelical churches today rarely have the same priority. Instead, there is a noticeable shift away from theology toward therapy, which is having disastrous effects on the lives of God's people and their families. The rock-solid foundation of the Word is now actively replaced by the shifting sand of man's philosophy, and believers are being washed out to sea. This swing away from a love for, and adherence to, absolute truth is documented by David Wells in his discerning critique of modern evangelicalism, *No Place for Truth, or, Whatever Happened to Evangelical Theology?* He says in his introduction,

> I have watched with growing disbelief as the evangelical Church has cheerfully plunged into astounding theological illiteracy. Many taking the plunge seem to imagine that they are simply following a path to success, but the effects of this great change in the evangelical soul are evident in every incoming class in the seminaries, in most publications, in the great majority of churches, and in most of their pastors. It is a change so large and so encompassing that those who dissent from what is happening are easily dismissed as individuals who cannot get along, who want to scruple over what is inconsequential, who are not loyal, and who are, in any case, quite irrelevant.[28]

Throughout his book, Wells offers examples of the shift away from a doctrinally based faith to an experience-based form of Christianity. One case in point exposes the church's preoccupation with self and therapy. This evaluation comes at the end of a thorough study of thirty years of the periodical *Christianity Today*, particularly the column "A Layman and His Faith":

> In these three decades [1959–1989], the laity had apparently moved from a doctrinally framed faith, the central concern of which was truth, to a therapeutically constructed faith, the central concern of which was psychological survival. Christian truth went from being an end in itself to being merely the means to personal healing. Thus was biblical truth eclipsed by the self and holiness by wholeness.[29]

As people's perceived psychological needs become more important than believing right doctrine, and feeling good about oneself becomes a higher priority than knowing one's soul is right with God, the systematic teaching of biblical doctrine becomes more important than ever. In fact, it is indispensable to the disciple-making process because of the power of doctrine to protect, build up, nourish believers, and stimulate spiritual growth (1 Tim. 4:6; 1 Peter 2:2). Conversely, bad doctrine has the power to undermine faith and damage believers if church shepherds are not discerning and consequently allow man-centered, Christianized self-help theory to permeate the church and thus redirect the eyes of believers off of Christ and onto self. That which common man may consider to be good psychology may in fact be nothing more than bad theology.

Bad theology is like poison that invades the bloodstream and destroys spiritual health. False doctrine kills the church from the inside out, whether it is preached openly from the pulpit or shared subtly in the counseling room. The apostles warned of these "destructive heresies" (2 Peter 2:1–3) that hold undiscerning believers "captive through philosophy and empty deception" (Col. 2:8). Therefore, church leaders must instruct men "not to teach strange doctrines" (1 Tim. 1:3) because "their talk will spread like gangrene" (2 Tim. 2:15–18). Gangrene is a deadly disease. Spreading throughout the skin tissue, it leaves portions of the body dead and in need of amputation. The disease starts when there is a lack of blood flow, and the resulting shortage of oxygen to the body parts causes tissue to die. Once dead, the tissue becomes numb and turns black, leaving only one effective treatment—removal of all dead tissue and the exposure of infected areas to oxygen under high pressure, thus killing the bacteria that can only live in oxygen-free tissue.

Consider this as an analogy of theology in the body of Christ, the church. Sound biblical doctrine, like oxygen, is needed to sustain spiritual life. When there is a lack of sound doctrine, the poison of false theories begins to spread underneath the surface of the skin until the infected area of the body dies. Once dead, it becomes numb to any danger. To remove false doctrine from the church requires amputation, followed by intense doses of pure doctrine to force the error out. Os Guinness reminds us that "sound doctrine" in Greek "is literally 'hygienic' and health-giving."[30] It cleanses the mind and feeds the growth of the body.

As authentic shepherds, therefore, we must make the imparting of doctrine a significant part of our teaching ministry. As believers are grounded in the Word of God and taught to think of everything in their lives from a God-centered, biblical perspective, their minds will be renewed and their faith nurtured (Rom. 12:1–2; 1 Tim. 4:6). Gary Johnson's comments are fitting: "A healthy Christianity cannot survive without theology, and theology must matter today, especially in our mindless and irrational culture. It should especially matter among evangelicals who confess saving attachment to Jesus Christ. But current challenges to the authority of the biblical gospel often come from within our churches, from practitioners who are increasingly uninterested in serious theology."[31] Therefore, if we are committed to biblical shepherding, we must take theology seriously, since the ongoing spiritual health and growth of our disciples depends upon it.

## WISE SHEPHERDING

The final characteristic of authentic ministry, as defined in Colossians 1:24–29, requires that we teach "with all wisdom." The Greek word translated "wisdom" is *sophia*, which refers to "the wisdom that is related to goodness, or to goodness itself as seen from one viewpoint, as the wisdom only the good can possess."[32] By choosing this word, Paul is making reference to the *manner* in which he carried out his ministry. In other words, he sought always to reflect the grace and goodness of God in how he treated people.

This kind of wisdom recognizes that not all disciples are ready for equal doses of theological truth. Jesus' teaching is an example for us to follow: "I have many more things to say to you, but you cannot bear them now" (John 16:12). The wise shepherd will not practice "dump-truck counseling." That is, he will not give someone "ten new things" to practice this week when making progress in one area may be all he or she can handle, and to make progress in that one area will bring the encouragement needed to move that person farther along.

As authentic ministers of the gospel, therefore, we must be wise. But that means more than being skillful, essential though that is; it also means that every word spoken to help or correct others is chosen for their good and reflects the mercy and patience of God. As shepherds, we must be the first to model Colossians 4:6: "Let your speech always be with grace, seasoned with salt, so that you will know how you should respond to each person."

The personality of faithful shepherding is multi-faceted like a gem. When held up to God's light, it reflects responsible stewardship, the humility of Jesus, dependence on the authority and power of Scripture, preoccupation with Christ, love that cares enough to correct, theological precision, and goodness in its treatment of both easy and difficult people. This is the model of shepherding we are called to follow.

## THE PURPOSE OF AUTHENTIC MINISTRY

The third element of biblically authentic ministry is its purpose, which is straightforwardly stated by Paul to be "that we may present every man complete in Christ" (Col. 1:28). The faithful shepherd labors intensely in his public teaching and personal ministry toward the goal of spiritual maturity in others while he pursues the same for himself.

The Greek word translated "complete" is *teleios*. According to *Synonyms of the New Testament*, "All of the various uses of *teleios* refer to the *telos*, which is its goal. In a natural sense the *teleioi* are adults who have attained their full stature, strength, and mental powers; they have attained their *telos*. Such adults are distinguished from the *neoi* or *paides*—young men or boys."[33] The word is sometimes translated "perfect" (e.g. Col. 4:12) but does not imply perfectionism. Richard Trench explains, "The faithful Christian is to be 'perfect' in the sense of striving by God's grace to be fully furnished and firmly established in the knowledge and practice of the things of God. Such 'perfection' refers to spiritual and moral maturity and is to be contrasted with the moral and spiritual condition of those who are babes in Christ."[34] Other uses of this word shed light on what this maturity looks like. For example, "mature" believers can handle solid meat because they are trained in discernment (Heb. 5:14); "perfect" believers are those who are not content with their spirituality but press on to greater Christlikeness (Phil. 3:15), and they are those who allow God-sent trials to produce endurance so that its "perfect" result of completeness can be obtained (James 1:4). What is especially thrilling about the goal of spiritual maturity is that it is God's goal for us as well as for those we are counseling. "And we know that God causes all things to work together for good to those who love God, to those who are called according to His purpose. For those whom He foreknew, He also predestined *to become conformed to the image of His Son*" (Rom. 8:28–29). We can be confident that His goal will be accomplished, since He not only began this good work in us and the believers to whom we minister, but also will "perfect it until the day of Christ Jesus" (Phil. 1:6).

Paul's goal of presenting believers as complete, or mature, reaches its end "in Christ." The embodiment of completeness is nothing other than Christlikeness. In other words, we are spiritually mature when we are fully like Jesus. Therefore, since no believer has yet to fully arrive at his or her *telos*, we as shepherds need to equip God's sheep toward "a mature man, to the measure of the stature which belongs to the fullness of Christ" (Eph. 4:13).

## THE PERSPIRATION OF AUTHENTIC MINISTRY

Fourth and last, authentic ministry requires tireless and tiring effort. The "perspiration" of shepherding is described thus: "For this purpose also I labor, striving according to His power, which mightily works within me" (Col. 1:29). "For this purpose," the goal of spiritual adulthood, Paul works himself to the point of fatigue. His "ministerial sweat" includes three qualities: intensive labor, active opposition, and divine enablement.

### Intensive labor

First, the word "labor" paints a picture of exhaustion. It comes from the word meaning "to grow weary or toil."[35] In other words, the apostle was so determined to meet his goal of presenting believers who were spiritually mature in Christ that he was willing to work to the point of physical, mental, and emotional weariness. Simon Peter uses the same word when he tells Jesus, "Master, we *worked hard* all night and caught nothing" (Luke 5:5). When Paul calls Timothy to "suffer hardship" as a good soldier of Christ, another analogy he uses is that of the "*hard-working* farmer" (2 Tim. 2:6). The overwhelming picture of ministry in the letters of Paul is not one of ease, comfort, and a secure retirement package, but of continuous hard labor and striving. However, as difficult as it is being a servant of the gospel, it is not gloom and drudgery to Paul and his coworkers, because they "fixed [their] hope on the living God, who is the Savior of all men, especially of believers" (1 Tim. 4:10). In his classic work, *The Christian Ministry*, Charles Bridges writes of the need for young men to realize the weight of pastoral ministry before entering it:

> [L]et every prospective view of the Ministry realize it as *an absorbing work*—as a high and holy vocation; involving results, which eternity alone can disclose, and therefore demanding the entire consecration of health, time, energy, and life itself to the accomplishment of its vast designs. If the soul be really engrossed with the mighty project of "saving souls from death," and *instrumentally* fixing them in the Redeemer's crown—how will every other object fade as a mere transient emotion—how will this great work of Preparation deepen in the sense of the responsibility! The one self-annihilating desire will be, that, whether our course be long or short—in joy or sorrow—in honour or dishonour—"we may so labour, that we may be accepted" of our Gracious Master.[36]

Anyone who considers giving his life to the work of shepherding must reckon with the reality that authentic ministry may cost a man his life. It will test his physical, mental, and emotional strength at levels he has never before known. He must, therefore, be willing to follow the example of Jesus, "who for the joy set before Him endured the cross" (Heb. 12:2).

## ACTIVE OPPOSITION

Second, the word "striving" indicates that real-life ministry among real-life sinners can sometimes seem like a wrestling match. Its Greek root, *agonizomai*, from which we get "agony" and "agonize," means to exert great effort. The *Linguistic Key to the Greek New Testament* says that this word especially emphasizes "Paul's missionary work, with all its attendant toil, its tireless exertion, and its struggles against all manner of setbacks and opposition."[37] Just a few verses later, Paul mentions the "struggle" he has had on the Colossians' behalf (Col. 2:1). Since he had not yet seen these believers face to face, his struggle for them must have included prayer (1:9–12). Therefore, ministry in the name of Christ is a constant spiritual struggle for the well-being of those under our care, whether we as shepherds are physically with the sheep or not.

Knowing this, we must also recognize that a large part of this struggle is the reality of spiritual warfare. Though we may feel that we are fighting people (often the very ones we want to help the most), our actual struggle "is not against flesh and blood, but against the rulers, against the powers, against the world forces of this darkness, against the spiritual forces of wickedness in the heavenly places" (Eph. 6:12). As we strive to come alongside in order to help others overcome sin and grow in their obedience to Christ, we certainly don't want to give Satan more credit than he deserves. However, we also want to guard against a shallow understanding of the conflict that is presently raging in the invisible world and thereby be tempted to find more humanly acceptable explanations for spiritual struggles. D. A. Carson challenges us with these words:

> The shallowness of spiritual conflict in the West owes something, no doubt, to centuries of Christian influence and the relentless exposure of superstition. But, less honorably,

> it also owes something, nowadays, to raw secularism, and a pervasive world view that thinks of all reality on a naturalistic plane. In other words, our failure to perceive more of what is going on in the demonic realm may sometimes owe less to our Christian heritage than to our deep indebtedness to a culture that assigns sociological, psychological, and economic reasons for everything.[38]

There is undoubtedly more spiritual warfare against those committed to biblical ministry than we realize. Our enemy has an agenda and it is not pretty: it is simply to devour disciples of Jesus (1 Peter 5:8). If we want to be used by God to make a difference in the lives of others for the sake of Christ, we must be prepared for active opposition from the devil and his demonic cohorts. Opposition, however, does sometimes have a human face. Paul's theology of spiritual warfare recognized that, though the power is invisible, the opponents often have real names, such as Hymenaeus, Alexander, or Philetus (1 Tim. 1:20; 2 Tim. 2:17).

### DIVINE ENABLEMENT

Third, although the effort required by authentic ministry involves intense labor and opposition, we may rest assured that God has provided every resource we need in order to be victorious through Him. We, like Paul, can be confident that we will reach our goal of helping others become like Christ through "His power, which mightily works within [us]" (Col. 1:29). This ability or might is the supernatural ability of the Holy Spirit working within disciple-makers, energizing us for our part in the process of sanctification.

## SUMMARY

There is a need for God's undershepherds to commit themselves to authentic ministry. The price is high: it is transparent suffering. The personality is comprehensive: it is suited to meet the real needs of every person. The purpose is definite: it is to become like Jesus. And the power is more than adequate: it is supernatural. The Holy

Spirit working within us as ministers makes us competent counselors and, therefore, useful tools in God's work of leading others toward spiritual maturity. However, the maturity that produces effective ministry does not take place in a vacuum. Instead, when we as church shepherds faithfully preach sound doctrine and consistently exemplify godly living, believers are equipped to help one another grow in Christlikeness. Therefore, we must now turn our attention to the crucial role of the pastor as a teaching shepherd who equips God's flock for effective service.

# Chapter Three:

# A Shepherd Equips God's Flock for Effective Service

*[Jesus gave] some as pastors and teachers, for the equipping of the saints for the work of service, to the building up of the body of Christ.*

*–Ephesians 4:12*

Authentic biblical shepherding works toward the goal of seeing the local church function as a healthy body of believers running the Christian race as a unified team while being intentionally equipped by Spirit-gifted men. As a result, each member is prepared to carry out his or her God-appointed role in the work of building up the whole church. God's vision of discipleship requires pastors to lead the work by faithfully teaching the Word in order to equip the members of the body in sound doctrine and godly living so that believers are able to counsel one another as loving amplifiers of the truth. Therefore, we must be committed to biblical church growth that is discontented with surface involvement from its members and instead deliberately focuses on their progressive sanctification toward maturity characterized by the servanthood of Jesus Christ. To pursue this strategy of discipleship, we must examine what genuine growth looks like from God's perspective, and particularly the role that church shepherds have in the process.

> And He gave some as apostles, and some as prophets, and some as evangelists, and some as pastors and teachers, for

> the equipping of the saints for the work of service, to the building up of the body of Christ; until we all attain to the unity of the faith, and of the knowledge of the Son of God, to a mature man, to the measure of the stature which belongs to the fullness of Christ. As a result, we are no longer to be children, tossed here and there by waves and carried about by every wind of doctrine, by the trickery of men, by craftiness in deceitful scheming; but speaking the truth in love, we are to grow up in all aspects into Him who is the head, even Christ, from whom the whole body, being fitted and held together by what every joint supplies, according to the proper working of each individual part, causes the growth of the body for the building up of itself in love.
>
> Eph. 4:11–16

A proper understanding of this passage begins with a brief look at its context. Ephesians 4 begins the application section of the book. Having spent three chapters teaching the great doctrines of Christ, salvation by grace, and the church, the apostle now exhorts us as disciples to live worthy of our high calling and position in the body of Christ. Verses 11–16 of that chapter complete a presentation of spiritual gifts that God has provided for the church's edification, specifically focusing on the gifted leadership He has given for the purpose of caring for believers and equipping them for everyday ministry. This, Paul teaches, is a crucial part of leading God's flock to spiritual maturity. Here we discover five elements of church growth from God's perspective.

## THE PROVISION FOR GROWTH

The first element of God's design for growth is His provision. Verse 11 begins with the conjunction "and," which connects this verse with the previous text. In addition to the spiritual gifts sovereignly granted to believers (Eph. 4:7–10), Jesus gave to the church gifted men, being part of "Christ's gift" (v. 7). Four categories of ministers are introduced. For our purpose in this chapter, we will briefly survey the first three while giving more concentrated attention to the fourth.

## Apostles

The first group of men given to the church consists of the apostles. The title "apostle" literally means "one sent on a mission."[1] According to *The Pulpit Commentary*, its primary use is in reference to the twelve apostles entrusted with laying the foundation of the church (see Eph. 2:20; 3:5):

> It is not meant that He gave to some the gifts needed to constitute them apostles, though that is true; but that, having qualified some to be apostles, He gave them to the Church. An apostle had his commission from Christ (Matt. 10:5); he possessed supernatural gifts (Matt. 10:8); it was necessary for him to have seen the Lord (Acts 1:22) … The apostles were the constituent body of the Church—they had all necessary gifts for setting it up, and as all Christian history has testified, they were a marvelous gift of Christ to his Church.[2]

Thus, "apostles" refers to that special group of men who were personally called by Jesus. This conclusion is supported by the account of how the eleven replaced Judas (Acts 1:15–26). Since Psalm 109:8 predicted that another man would replace the betrayer, this Old Testament truth is quoted when Peter announced to the disciples, "Therefore it is necessary" that another one "must become a witness with us of His resurrection" (vv. 21–22). Luke 22:28–30 predicted the apostles' unique role in the future kingdom as judges of the twelve tribes of Israel. So, with Judas gone, a twelfth man was needed. However, there were two specific qualifications the substitute had to meet (v. 22). He had to be both an eyewitness of the earthly life and ministry of Christ ("accompanied us all the time"), as well as be a "witness with us of His resurrection." Only two men met those requirements: Joseph called Barsabbas, and Matthias. So they prayed, cast lots, and determined the Lord's choice to be Matthias. Thus the apostolic team was again complete.

## Prophets

Second, "prophets" were given to edify the church. In New Testament times, this term referred not only to those who foretold the future, but also to those who forthrightly preached messages from God. The Greek word literally means "one who speaks forth or openly."[3] New Testament prophets were essential before the Scriptures were complete; however, once the written revelation of God was finished, the church had an infallible guide to His will and prophets were no longer needed. "God, after He spoke long ago to the fathers in the prophets in many portions and in many ways, in these last days has spoken to us in His Son, whom He appointed heir of all things, through whom also He made the world" (Heb. 1:1–2). Jesus Christ, the incarnate Word, revealed God to men, and that final revelation is now found in the written Word of God, the Bible. As Jesus promised, the Holy Spirit is now our Teacher, helping us understand the Word so that we can teach others "all that [He] commanded" (John 14:26; Matt. 28:20).

God also made it clear that His revelation was complete when He gave strong warnings to anyone who would add to or subtract from it:

> I testify to everyone who hears the words of the prophecy of this book: if anyone adds to them, God will add to him the plagues which are written in this book; and if anyone takes away from the words of the book of this prophecy, God will take away his part from the tree of life and from the holy city, which are written in this book.
>
> Rev. 22:18–19

Someone may argue, "But it says, 'this book'; therefore the warning only pertains to Revelation." However, that conclusion is inadequate for two reasons. First, since the Holy Spirit guided the process of the inscripturation of the Word (2 Peter 1:19–21), it is no accident that the book of Revelation appears last. Thus the warning extends backward all the way to Genesis. Second, this was not the first time God gave this word of warning. Proverbs 30:5–6 says, "Every word of God is tested; He is a shield to those who take refuge in Him.

Do not add to His words or He will reprove you, and you will be proved a liar." God is not giving any new revelation today. His Word is complete. The canon of Scripture is closed. Now the task of His shepherds is to proclaim it and teach people how to live it. Therefore, there are no apostles and prophets in the church today; however, there are pastors who speak prophetically. They do not foretell the future but, as a result of keen discernment, wisdom, and knowledge of the Word of God, they carry a burden to warn God's church forthrightly of the subtle intrusion of false philosophies and doctrines. When Bible teachers defend the written Word by sounding the trumpet as guardians of the truth, there is a sense in which they are being prophetic (e.g. 1 Tim. 1:3; 4:6; 6:3, 20; 2 Tim. 1:13–14; 4:1–4; Titus 1:9; 2:1).

### EVANGELISTS

The third group of gifted men is referred to as "evangelists." As John MacArthur notes, a biblical evangelist "is not a man with ten suits and ten sermons who runs a road show."[4] Rather, an evangelist in Paul's day "was one who proclaimed the gospel, which he had received from the apostle. He was particularly a missionary who brought the gospel into new regions."[5] Therefore, a biblical evangelist, or missionary pastor, is one who goes into uncharted territory with the goal of planting an indigenous Bible-preaching local church. The Apostle Paul shared this pioneering spirit: "And thus I aspired to preach the gospel, not where Christ was already named, so that I would not build on another man's foundation" (Rom. 15:20).

The term is used only two other times in the New Testament: first, in reference to "Philip the evangelist" who took the gospel to the region of Samaria (Acts 21:8; 8:5); second, when Timothy was told to "do the work of an evangelist," becoming a prototype for all future pastors faithfully preaching the Word evangelistically (2 Tim. 4:5). As the gospel with all its practical implications is preached, disciples are born and local churches are planted in order to carry the reproductive work further to the ends of the earth. Until "the fullness of the Gentiles has come in" (Rom. 11:25), the church will need many servants to be involved in the work of biblical evangelism and missionary outreach.

## PASTOR-TEACHERS

The fourth group of spiritually gifted men is that of "pastors and teachers," and it is this role that is of particular interest in this chapter because the weight of Bible teaching rests primarily on the shoulders of these men. The absence of the definite article between the two titles indicates that it refers to one person: a pastor-teacher. The Greek word *poimain* means "shepherd" and *didaskalous* means "teachers"; together the terms literally mean "teaching shepherds"[6] (compare 1 Tim. 3:2; Titus 1:9). Greek scholar Kenneth Wuest writes, "God's ideal pastor is one who engages in a didactic [teaching] ministry, feeding the saints on expository preaching, giving them the rich food of the Word."[7] Though Christians today have all sorts of ideas of what a pastor is to do and be, shepherds must choose first to immerse themselves in the study of Scripture in order to feed and care for God's sheep. As John Stott writes,

> If today's pastors were to take seriously the New Testament emphasis on the priority of preaching and teaching, not only would they find it extremely fulfilling themselves, but also it would undoubtedly have a very wholesome effect on the Church. Instead, tragic to relate, many are essentially administrators, whose symbols of ministry are the office rather than the study, and the telephone rather than the Bible.[8]

To some degree, an abundance of professional counseling exists within Christianity because passionate, expositional, theological preaching that relentlessly exhorts its listeners to obey Jesus Christ does not. This sounds like a sweeping statement and runs the risk of laying all the blame for believers' personal problems on the failure of pulpit ministry. But that is not my intent. However, I do mean to make it inescapably clear that nothing can or should ever replace the exalted position of teaching and preaching the Word of God in the life and ministry of the local church. A biblical counseling/

soul care ministry will not be effective in churches whose pastors are unfaithful in the pulpit. In other words, discipling one another works best when it is built upon, and flows from, an undying commitment to faithful, biblical preaching. When this kind of preaching is regularly fed to God's sheep, and the Word is habitually applied to their lives by faithful shepherds who also model a commitment to the personal ministry of the Word, followers of Jesus will make progress in their sanctification. John Shaw refers to pastors like these as gifts from God. In *The Character of a Pastor According to God's Heart*, he makes the following comments:

> With respect to such pastors, it is God who raises them up, and qualifies and prepares them for the high and sacred office of the ministry. He orders the time and place of their birth; the means, opportunities, and advantages of their education. It is God who apprehends them by His Spirit and grace, forming Christ in their hearts, and setting up His spiritual kingdom there … That bias upon their hearts to enter upon the work of the ministry is of God's forming, and so is that upon the hearts of a people by whom they are invited and called, to take the pastoral care and charge of them in the Lord.[9]

God's provision of men like this is for the spiritual growth of the people whom He calls to Himself for the purpose of glorifying Jesus Christ.

## THE PROGRESSION OF GROWTH

The second element of God's design for church growth is the product of His gracious provision. In Ephesians 4:12, the Apostle Paul explains a three-step progression toward maturity.

### EQUIPPING

Spiritually gifted men are given to the church first "for the equipping of the saints." In Matthew 4:21, the word *katartismos* is used in reference to "mending" fishing nets. Just as Peter made his nets ready for his occupation, so pastors prepare God's people to serve the Lord as effective fishers of men. When disciples are trained to submit to the Lordship of Christ in their daily lives, they are made ready "to make a defense to everyone who asks [them] to give an account for the hope that is in [them], yet with gentleness and reverence" (1 Peter 3:15).

However, "equipping" is, in the original Greek, primarily a technical medical term referring to "the setting of a bone."[10] A form of the word is used in Galatians 6:1 in this sense, where it refers to the loving restoration of a sinning brother to proper usefulness in the body of Christ: "Brethren, even if anyone is caught in any trespass, you who are spiritual, *restore* such a one." Though this is a ministry obligation for every member of the body,[11] it is obvious that pastors must take the lead in this personal, restorative, helping ministry. It is part of the equipping process. In this regard, Richard Baxter's counsel is again appreciated:

> A minister is not to be merely a public preacher, but to be known as a counsellor for their souls, as the physician is for their bodies, and the lawyer for their estates: so that each man who is in doubts and straits, may bring his case to him for resolution; as Nicodemus came to Christ, and as it was usual with the people of old to go to the priest … [As] the people have become unacquainted with this office of the ministry, and with their own duty and necessity in this respect, it belongeth to us to acquaint them with it, and publicly to press them to come to us for advice about the great concerns of their souls. We must not only be willing to take the trouble, but should draw it upon ourselves, by inviting them to come. What abundance of good might we do, could we but bring them to this! … One word of seasonable, prudent advice, given by a minister to persons in necessity, may be of more use than many sermons.[12]

When nets get torn, someone needs to re-stitch them. When bones are broken, a physician needs to see that they are properly set back in place. When sheep stumble, a shepherd needs to care for them by helping them to get back up and function effectively in the fellowship of God's pasture.

## Service

The second step in this progression of growth is for disciples to be equipped "for the work of service." The word translated "service" is related to *diakonos*, from which we get "deacon." However, of the thirty times this word is used in the New Testament, only in five does it refer to an official church office (Phil. 1:1; 1 Tim. 3:8–13); everywhere else it is "ministers" or "servants." In other words, the church is not built by one man, or even a few men, but by every believer being actively involved in ministry through evangelizing the lost people in their lives and serving their fellow Christians. Consider the discipleship that would naturally take place in the life of a local church if every believer would practice the one-another ministry that the early churches first read about in the instructions they received from the apostles:

- Be devoted to one another (Rom. 12:10).
- Give preference to one another (Rom. 12:10).
- Be of the same mind toward one another (Rom. 12:16).
- Accept one another by withholding judgment (Rom. 14:1).
- Accept one another by showing deference (Rom. 14:1–5; 15:7).
- Esteem [highly regard] one another in love (Rom. 14:5; Phil. 2:3).
- Build up one another (Rom. 14:19; 1 Thes. 5:11).
- Serve one another by showing deference in matters of liberty (Gal. 5:13).
- Bear one another's sin burdens (Gal. 6:2).
- Be gentle with one another (Eph. 4:2).
- Be kind to one another so as to preserve unity (Eph. 4:32).
- Speak truth to one another (Eph. 4:25; Col 3:9).

- Submit to one another (Eph. 5:21).
- Show compassion to one another (Col. 3:12).
- Bear with the inherent sinfulness of one another (Col. 3:13).
- Forgive one another (Col. 3:13).
- Use Spirit-filled, Word-saturated music to teach and admonish one another (Col. 3:16; Eph. 5:19).
- Comfort one another with the hope of Christ's return (1 Thes. 4:18).
- Encourage one another (1 Thes. 5:11).
- Live in peace with one another (1 Thes. 5:13).
- Seek good for one another (1 Thes. 5:15).
- Encourage one another to forsake unbelief and hardness of heart (Heb. 3:13).
- Stimulate one another to spiritual growth (Heb. 10:24).
- Encourage one another by faithful participation in the church (Heb. 10:25).
- Confess sins to one another (James 5:16).
- Pray for one another's spiritual and physical healing (James 5:16).
- Be long-suffering and patient toward one another (1 Peter 4:8; Eph. 4:2).
- Be hospitable to one another without complaint (1 Peter 4:9).
- Serve one another (1 Peter 4:10; Gal. 5:13).
- Act in humility toward one another (1 Peter 5:5).
- Show holy affection to one another (1 Peter 5:14).
- Participate in the holy walk with one another (1 John 1:7).
- Love one another by refusing to become resentful (1 John 3:11–12).

- Love one another by giving sacrificially to meet others' needs (1 John 3:16–17).
- Love one another by fighting fears together (1 John 4:18).
- Love one another by walking in truth together (1 John 3:18; 2 John 1:5).

As shepherds, we have the responsibility to teach and train believers to make loving service to one another the normal Christian life. That is how disciples grow. It is also a powerful evangelistic tool, as Jesus says: "By this all men will know that you are My disciples, if you have love for one another" (John 13:35).

### BUILDING UP

The third step in the progression of growth is the goal of the "building up of the body of Christ" (Eph. 4:12). The word translated "building up" is a compound of the words for "house" and "to build" and is "used figuratively in the NT in the sense of edification, the promotion of spiritual growth."[13] Paul writes to the Corinthian church, "we are God's fellow workers; you are God's field, God's building" (1 Cor. 3:9). In other words, God wants all believers to help one another build the edifice of a working faith into each other's hearts and lives. We have been called to "please [our] neighbor for his good, to his edification" (Rom 15:2). This is the God-ordained means by which we will reach the goal of presenting "every man complete in Christ" (Col. 1:28).

As equipping shepherds, therefore, we must be committed to the priority of teaching the Word publicly from the pulpit and privately through the personal ministry of caring for souls. Only then will members of the body make progress in being fully prepared, and restored when necessary, to carry on the work of serving one another for the edification of all.

## THE PURPOSE FOR GROWTH

The progression of growth is to continue "until we all attain to the unity of the faith, and of the knowledge of the Son of God, to a mature man, to the measure of the stature which belongs to the fullness of Christ" (Eph. 4:13). "Attain" comes from a Greek word which means "to come down to the goal."[14] Therefore, the third element in God's design for growth is its purpose of attaining to the unity of the faith, spiritual maturity, and Christlikeness.

### UNITY OF THE FAITH AND KNOWLEDGE

First, biblical unity is that which is based upon "the faith," that is, the whole body of truth revealed in the Scriptures (see Acts 6:7; 14:22; Gal. 1:23; Jude 3). Genuine growth does not sacrifice truth in order to expand its influence. True Christian unity is not based upon issues of personal conviction, which often divide believers, but upon fundamental doctrines that unite those who love truth. God's ultimate goal for His church includes "being diligent to preserve the unity of the Spirit in the bond of peace" (Eph. 4:3). However, this is a call to preserve a Christ-centered unity, not to create a false version of it. Therefore, Paul teaches that biblical unity requires mutual "knowledge of the Son of God." "Knowledge" refers to "exact or full knowledge, discernment, recognition."[15] In other words, the kind of knowledge that maturity displays is the mutual love and exaltation of Jesus Christ as Lord in the daily lives of His disciples, which is evidenced by their love and care for one another within the realm of truth.

### MATURE MAN

Second, growth is to continue until we become spiritually reproductive adults. As we saw in the previous chapter, "mature" (*telios*) refers to that which is complete, full grown, "that which has reached the set goal."[16] The author of Hebrews provides an illustration of this kind of truth-based development when he expresses regret over his readers' spiritual immaturity:

> For though by this time you ought to be teachers, you have need again for someone to teach you the elementary principles of the oracles of God, and you have come to need milk and not solid food. For everyone who partakes only of

> milk is not accustomed to the word of righteousness, for he is an infant. But solid food is for the mature, who because of practice have their senses trained to discern good and evil.
>
> 5:12–14

The reason why the writer is so disappointed is because these believers have received plenty of sound teaching but have failed to apply it to their daily lives and, as a result, they are still spiritual infants who cannot handle chewing the juicy steak of theology. Instead, they need someone to continue spoon-feeding them strained mush or to hold their milk bottle while being coddled. Clearly, one of the marks of spiritual growth is the ability to take in the Word of God and chew on it mentally so as to grow in the ability to discern the philosophies of men. The more disciples are trained in the daily application of biblical truth to life, the more spiritually reproductive they will be.

### MEASURE OF THE STATURE OF CHRIST

Third, God measures church growth on the basis of progress toward "the measure of the stature which belongs to the fullness of Christ." This phrase repeats the previous idea of being full grown but draws attention to the specific pattern to follow—Jesus Christ. Biblical sanctification does not aim at becoming a carbon copy of another Christian but instead imitating the "fullness of Christ"—all He is, His virtues, and His holy love. Paul regularly pleaded with God to produce this in disciples when he prayed for them "to know the love of Christ which surpasses knowledge, that [they] may be filled up to all the fullness of God" (Eph. 3:19). He also thanked God for the Thessalonians' productivity, since their maturity enabled them to become "an example [pattern] to all the believers in Macedonia and in Achaia" (1 Thes. 1:7).

This is the kind of maturity that God desires as He persistently works His agenda of conforming believers to the image of Christ (Rom. 8:29). As equipping pastors, therefore, we must actively resist worldly measurements of success and instead constantly work in cooperation with God's design for growth. As disciples grow in their faith and knowledge of Him, they will become spiritually reproductive, obedient followers of Jesus.

## THE PROOF OF GROWTH

The fourth element of genuine growth is its evidence. As pastor-teachers faithfully use the Word of God to lead believers toward Christlikeness, two marks of maturity will become apparent: doctrinal stability and a faithful testimony (Eph. 4:14–15).

### DOCTRINAL STABILITY

First, disciples are "no longer to be children," or, as Curtis Vaughan says, "infants at the mercy of error."[17] "Children" literally refers to babies: "It refers to the immaturity of children in opposition to the perfection of the perfect man."[18] Immature believers are often theologically unstable. They are easily "tossed here and there by waves" and "carried about by every wind of doctrine," and often resemble the man lacking wise faith who, like the surf of the sea, is "driven and tossed by the wind" (James 1:6). The teachings of men blow infantile believers around in circles, chasing after the latest spiritual trend because they are naïve and easily fall prey to "the trickery of men." William Hendricksen explains,

> The term "trickery," applied to those who in effect were attempting to lead believers astray, is *kubeia*, from *kubos*, meaning *cube*, *die*. Paul is thinking, therefore, of *dice-playing* in which tricks were used in order to win. Hence, the word came to mean *trickery*; here "human trickery," the talent literally, readiness to do anything for deceitful scheming.[19]

A lack of growth in sound doctrine causes believers to fall prey to false teachers by being carried away by "craftiness in deceitful scheming." They are deceived by charlatans whose "unscrupulous conduct"[20] and cunning methods ensnare their victims. As a result, people wander from the truth. But maturity in doctrinal understanding will protect God's sheep from religious con men.

I am convinced that the weakness of too many pulpits is a primary cause of the widespread doctrinal immaturity present in today's professing church. Therefore, the fault must be laid at the door of pastors. Steven Lawson shares my concern over this famine in our lands in his outstanding book on expository preaching:

> Tragically, most of what passes for biblical preaching today falls woefully short of apostolic standards. Many pastors seem content to dole out pabulum to spiritual babies instead of teaching the full counsel of God. Many evangelical ministers have succumbed to delivering secular-sounding, motivational pep talks aimed at soothing the felt needs of restless church shoppers or, worse, salving the guilty consciences of unregenerate church members. Rather than expounding the depths of God's Word, many Bible-believing ministers have chosen the path of least resistance, content to scratch the surface of shallow souls and tickle the ears of languid listeners. The result is congregations are starving—even though many of the famished may not be aware of it—settling for sickly sweet, yet totally inadequate, spiritual pabulum.[21]

If, by God's grace, we are to have the privilege of seeing any measurable growth toward spiritual maturity and doctrinal discernment among believers today, we as church shepherds must plead with God to widen our shoulders in order to faithfully carry out the responsibility that rests squarely upon us. Believers must also stop believing everything they hear and start testing the teachings of men (1 John 4:1). Then, and only then, will disciples begin to show evidence of doctrinal stability.

## FAITHFUL TESTIMONY

Second, spiritual maturity is evidenced by integrity in proclamation. Unlike the immature, who are easily led astray by false teaching of various sorts, mature believers are committed to truthful speech and conduct. "Speaking the truth in love" is a present-tense participle indicating continuous action and could be translated, "truthing in love." Martyn Lloyd-Jones refers to this as "not a pleasant" translation, adding,

> What the expression conveys is that we are "in the truth" and that we are "walking in the truth." Perhaps the best translation of all would be "having or holding the truth in love." That, of course, includes speaking it, and discussing it together, and teaching it. But it is not merely speaking; it covers the whole of our deportment. We are to be true and to walk in the truth and in love.[22]

Another commentator writes, "Truth is the element in which we are to live, move, and have our being; fidelity to truth is the backbone of the Christian ministry."[23] Applying this principle to the ministry of counseling in the church, Powlison argues,

> In modern America, the "mental health system" is a vast complex of higher education, hospitals, publishers, third-party insurers, drug companies, licensing boards, and private practice psychotherapists. But the loving truth and truthful love of Ephesians 4:15 come embedded in a different social system: the *ekklesia* of the people of God … God's new society in Christ, come into its own and coming into its own, is *the* institution for counseling ministry.[24]

By walking in the truth, we "grow up in all aspects." God desires all believers to experience a continual increase in spirituality in respect to all things; in other words, total growth. Peter calls for this kind of well-rounded development in his second letter:

> Grace and peace be multiplied to you in the knowledge of God and of Jesus our Lord; seeing that His divine power has granted to us everything pertaining to life and godliness, through the true knowledge of Him who called us by His own glory and excellence. For by these He has granted to us His precious and magnificent promises, so that by them you may become partakers of the divine nature, having escaped

> the corruption that is in the world by lust. Now for this very reason also, applying all diligence, in your faith supply moral excellence, and in your moral excellence, knowledge, and in your knowledge, self-control, and in your self-control, perseverance, and in your perseverance, godliness, and in your godliness, brotherly kindness, and in your brotherly kindness, love. For if these qualities are yours and are increasing, they render you neither useless nor unfruitful in the true knowledge of our Lord Jesus Christ.
>
> 2 Pet. 1:2–8

By His grace, God has given the disciple of Christ "everything pertaining to life and godliness." There is nothing needed outside the gracious provision He has made in His Word, the Spirit, and the community of faith known as the church. As believers diligently apply God's resources, the attractive growth Peter describes will be manifested. Moral excellence, knowledge, self-control, perseverance, godliness, brotherly kindness, and love will increasingly be theirs and they will "adorn the doctrine of God" (Titus 2:10). As a result, maturing believers become living billboards for Christ, and the work of the gospel prospers. This kind of growth is "into Him who is the head, even Christ" (Eph. 4:15); that is, the ultimate goal of the body is to follow the leadership of the Head. He is our example and, therefore, the One after whom we must pattern our lives (see Heb. 12:2; Eph. 1:22–23; Col. 1:18).

## THE POWER FOR GROWTH

The fifth element of God's design for church growth is the power that produces the increase (Eph. 4:16). As the Head, Christ is the source "from whom the whole body" receives its energy and is "being fitted and held together." The word translated "fitted" is, in the Greek, a present participle meaning "to fit or frame together,"[25] while "held together" means "to bring together, unite,"[26] and refers to "a body which is held together by sinews, ligaments, and joints."[27] In other words, the church is not an organization but a functioning organism, a body (see Eph. 2:20–22). Both these verbs are passive, indicating that Jesus is the sovereign designer and builder, and we are the ligaments and muscles.

Just as the all-wise Creator knits human beings together in the womb (Ps. 139:13), so He weaves the individual parts of the body of Christ together into a living, functioning entity. Jesus, the master craftsman, does this "by what every joint supplies, according to the proper working of each individual part." The word "joint" refers to "contact with the supply."[28] The extent to which the energy of Christ is utilized depends upon the yielded faith of each member, which keeps him or her connected in vibrant fellowship with the Savior. Jesus says, "I am the vine, you are the branches; he who abides in Me and I in him, he bears much fruit, for apart from Me you can do nothing" (John 15:5). As each believer abides in Christ and works properly in the body of Christ, it "causes the growth of the body for the building up of itself in love."

## SUMMARY

Contrary to the latest marketing strategies that guarantee pastors instant numerical success, God's design for the growth of the church is the hard work of discipleship. This labor is characterized by the progressive maturing of believers in Christ, who learn to govern their lives by sound doctrine, to obey Christ, and to serve one another in love. A key ingredient in this kind of growth is the spiritual care of equipping pastors who are not content with church members warming pews, but instead tirelessly give themselves to the work of publicly teaching the Word and personally training disciples in sound doctrine and God-honoring living toward the goal of the entire body becoming like Christ. As church shepherds model this serious kind of approach to discipleship, believers are adequately prepared to discipline themselves for the ongoing battle against sin and are equipped for a life of effective service to the rest of God's flock.

# Chapter Four:

# A SHEPHERD SERVES FOR AN ETERNAL REWARD

*And when the Chief Shepherd appears, you will receive the unfading crown of glory.*

*–1 Peter 5:4*

Spiritual leadership is serious business reserved for serious men. It is serious business because we keep watch over souls "as those who will give an account" (Heb. 13:17). The knowledge of a future day of accountability, when the ministry of teaching shepherds will be judged by Christ, the Lord of the church, should cause every minister to approach his God-given responsibility with great zeal and sobriety. This is a proper and biblical motivation for faithful service, as Peter's charge to his fellow elders clearly indicates:

> … shepherd the flock of God among you, exercising oversight not under compulsion, but voluntarily, according to the will of God; and not for sordid gain, but with eagerness; nor yet as lording it over those allotted to your charge, but proving to be examples to the flock. And when the Chief Shepherd appears, you will receive the unfading crown of glory.
>
> 1 Peter 5:1–4

## THREE CHARACTERISTICS

The call to church shepherds is to exercise "oversight." Shepherds do not *take* authority that belongs to another, but they *exercise* their God-given responsibility as His overseers. This local-church oversight belongs not to the majority, but to certain qualified spiritual leaders who are appointed by God to watch over His sheep. Peter gives three characteristics of this ministry. Here we find a description of what spiritual oversight should look like in God's church.

### NOT UNDER COMPULSION, BUT VOLUNTARILY

First, the ministry of shepherding should flow from a willing heart, "voluntarily" rather than because of outward "compulsion." Church shepherds must be in their position "according to the will of God." In other words, we must be men who are not forced into leadership by some outside source such as family or friends, or simply because no one else will do it, but because we are inwardly convinced that it is God's calling for us. This, of course, does not negate the importance of having our calling and giftedness confirmed by others, but the fact remains that shepherds must lead willingly because of a desire to serve God and His people. Christ is the perfect example of voluntary service that flows from humility of mind:

> Have this attitude in yourselves which was also in Christ Jesus, who, although He existed in the form of God, did not regard equality with God a thing to be grasped, but emptied Himself, taking the form of a bond-servant, and being made in the likeness of men. And being found in appearance as a man, He humbled Himself by becoming obedient to the point of death, even death on a cross.
>
> Phil. 2:5–8

Christ was not pressured to serve. Yes, it was the Father's will that He should take upon Himself human flesh and die as the substitute for our sins (Heb. 10:5), but His ministry was no less voluntary. He served on His own accord. Likewise, spiritual leaders must be men who are thrust into leadership by an inner "Holy Spirit compulsion." They must shepherd the flock because they desire the work (1 Tim. 3:1). Louis Barbieri comments, "Because the position of shepherd includes problems as well as joys, the one who labors simply under a human call will soon quit the flock. The faithful shepherd is one who has responded with a willing heart to God's call to the job of shepherding."[1]

### NOT FOR SORDID GAIN, BUT WITH EAGERNESS

Second, the ministry of church oversight should be performed with enthusiasm for the work itself rather than with a carnal motive for financial gain at the expense of others. "Sordid gain" refers to a fondness for dishonest gain, that is, to go about something "greedily."[2] This was certainly a problem among the leaders in Judah: "from the least even to the greatest everyone is greedy for gain; from the prophet even to the priest everyone practices deceit" (Jer. 8:10). Titus 1:7 insists that a church overseer be "not fond of sordid gain." The implication is clear. A leader who is truly called by God is not driven by love for money, but is motivated by an inner zeal to do His work. However, this does not prohibit proper remuneration for ministers of the gospel. In fact, Paul writes, "The elders who rule well are to be considered worthy of double honor, especially those who work hard at preaching and teaching. For the Scripture says, 'You shall not muzzle the ox while he is threshing,' and 'The laborer is worthy of his wages'" (1 Tim. 5:17–18). A faithful shepherd is worthy of generous financial support, but this compensation must not be what ultimately drives him.

### NOT LORDING IT OVER, BUT PROVING TO BE EXAMPLES

Third, spiritual oversight is to be exercised in a spirit of humility and servanthood. The phrase "not lording it over" is sometimes translated "domineering," and means "forcefully ruling over."[3] Leaders who lord it over others strive to gain dominion by subduing those beneath them in order to exercise complete control. This is the character trait made famous by Diotrephes, who loved to "be first among them" (3 John 9). Jesus warns His disciples against this worldly form of leadership:

> But Jesus called them to Himself and said, "You know that the rulers of the Gentiles lord it over them, and their great men exercise authority over them. It is not this way among you, but whoever wishes to become great among you shall be your servant, and whoever wishes to be first among you shall be your slave; just as the Son of Man did not come to be served, but to serve, and to give His life a ransom for many."
>
> Matt. 20:25–28

As faithful shepherds, we care for the flock that is "allotted" to our charge (1 Peter 5:3). In other words, it is the flock portioned out by God to our care. This emphasizes both sovereignty and stewardship. Like the Ephesian elders, we must take care of "the church of God" (Acts 20:28). To realize that we do not care for our own churches but for the church that God purchased for Himself with the blood of His Son is sobering and raises enormous implications for how we "do church."

Rather than practicing tyrannical leadership, church shepherds are to be proving themselves to be examples. The word "example" refers to a pattern. Kenneth Wuest says it means "a print left as an impression after a blow."[4] Combined with the present participle translated "proving," the text literally reads, "You yourselves constantly be becoming a pattern for others to follow." In other words, the spiritual leader is to be the kind of person after whom believers can trace their lives. Paul exhorts Titus, "In all things show yourself to *be an example of good deeds*, with purity in doctrine, dignified" (Titus 2:7). Paul not only taught this, but also he modeled practical godliness to the extent that he could write to the Philippians, "Brethren, join in following my example, and observe those who walk according to the pattern you have in us" (Phil. 3:17).

To a great extent, the growth of God's flock depends upon the example of its shepherds. Oswald Sanders writes, "Water rises no higher than its source,"[5] and, "It is a general principle that we can influence and lead others only so far as we ourselves have gone. The person most likely to be successful is one who leads not by merely pointing the way but by having trodden it himself. We are leaders to the extent that we inspire others to follow us."[6] The shepherd's walk must match his talk for his ministry to experience God's fullest blessing. John Stott writes, "We cannot hide what we are. Indeed, what we are speaks as plainly as what we say. When these two voices blend, the impact of the message is doubled. But when they contradict each other, even the positive witness of the one is negated by the other."[7] We must take heed to the exhortation: "Let no one look down on your youthfulness, but rather in speech, conduct, love, faith and purity, *show yourself an example* of those who believe" (1 Tim. 4:12).

## ONE REWARD

Pastor-elders who are faithful in shepherding and overseeing God's flock can look forward to a reward when "the Chief Shepherd" appears (1 Peter 5:4). This title could be translated "Master Shepherd," which emphasizes the accountability of earthly shepherds to Christ, our Master. The word "appears" does not mean to become temporarily visible, but to be manifested in His true character. So when Christ manifests Himself in all His glory, His faithful undershepherds will receive the "unfading crown of glory," a reward that "will not fade away" (1 Peter 1:4), an eternal crown. The prize that Jesus will give to His faithful undershepherds will not be like the one given at the Olympic games, which was made of flowers that quickly withered; instead, their reward will last forever.

The faithful pastor will realize that his toil is not in vain when he keeps this eternal perspective. Though he may never receive due honor from the sheep he so faithfully serves in this life, his work will not go unnoticed or unrewarded by the Lord Jesus Christ. The reward he receives will far outweigh the sacrificial service he has offered to the church in the name of the One who gave His blood to purchase her. Sadly, as A. B. Simpson recognizes, "Often the crowd does not recognize a leader until he has gone, and then they build a monument for him with the stones they threw at him in life."[8] Though this may be the case for too many ministers, the faithful church shepherd will receive his just reward at the Second Coming of Christ. He will hear the words, "Well done, good and faithful slave" (Matt. 25:23). No greater compensation can be received. No greater commendation should be sought.

## FOR FURTHER HELP AND INFORMATION

### **BOOKS TO STRENGTHEN PERSONAL DISCIPLESHIP**


Adams, Jay E., *Christ and Your Problems* (Phillipsburg, NJ: P&R, 1971).

——*The Christian Counselor's Manual* (Grand Rapids, MI: Zondervan, 1973).

——*Competent to Counsel* (Grand Rapids, MI: Zondervan, 1970).

——*A Theology of Counseling* (Grand Rapids, MI: Zondervan, 1979).

——(ed.) *The Journal of Modern Ministry* (2004–2008).

Berg, Jim, *Changed Into His Image* (Greenville, SC: Bob Jones University Press, 2018).

Bobgan, Martin and Deidre, *How to Counsel from Scripture* (Chicago: Moody Press, 1985).

Bridges, Charles, *The Christian Ministry* (1830; 1967, Edinburgh: Banner of Truth).

Bridges, Jerry, *The Practice of Godliness* (Colorado Springs, CO: NavPress, 1983).

——*The Pursuit of Holiness* (Colorado Springs, CO: NavPress, 1978).

——*Trusting God* (Colorado Springs, CO: NavPress, 1988).

Coleman, Robert E., *The Master Plan of Evangelism* (Old Tappan, NJ: Fleming H. Revell, 1963).

DeMoss, Nancy Leigh, *Lies Women Believe* (Chicago: Moody Press, 2001).

Fitzpatrick, Elyse, and Hendricksen, M.D., Laura, *Will Medicine Stop the Pain?* (Chicago: Moody Press, 2006).

—— and Carol Cornish, (eds.), *Women Helping Women* (Eugene, OR: Harvest House, 1997).

Gallagher, Steve, *At the Altar of Sexual Idolatry* (Dry Ridge, KY: Pure Life Ministries, 2000).

Hughes, Barbara, *Disciplines of a Godly Woman* (Wheaton, IL: Crossway, 2001).

Hughes, R. Kent, *Disciplines of a Godly Man* (Wheaton, IL: Crossway, 1991).

Hull, Bill, *The Disciple Making Pastor* (Grand Rapids, MI: Fleming H. Revell, 1988).

Johnson, Eric L., and Jones, Stanton L., (eds.), *Psychology and Christianity: Four Views* (Downers Grove, IL: IVP Academic, 2000).

Lane, Timothy S., and Tripp, Paul David, *How People Change* (Greensboro, NC: New Growth Press, 2008).

Lloyd-Jones, D. Martyn, *Spiritual Depression: Its Causes and Cure* (Grand Rapids, MI: Eerdmans, 1965).

MacArthur, John F., *Our Sufficiency in Christ* (Dallas: Word, 1991).

——and The Master's Seminary Faculty, *Counseling* (Nashville: Thomas Nelson, 2005).

MacDonald, James, *I Want to Change … So, Help Me God* (Chicago: Moody Press, 2000).

Mack, Wayne, *A Homework Manual for Biblical Counseling* (Phillipsburg, NJ: P&R, 1977).

——*Your Family God's Way* (Phillipsburg, NJ: P&R, 1991).

Mahaney, C. J., *The Cross Centered Life* (Sisters, OR: Multnomah, 2002).

Powlison, David, *Seeing with New Eyes* (Phillipsburg, NJ: P&R, 2003).

——*Speaking Truth in Love: Counsel in Community* (Winston-Salem, NC: Punch Press, 2005).

Priolo, Lou, *The Heart of Anger* (Amityville, NY: Calvary Press, 1997).

——*Pleasing People* (Phillipsburg, NJ: P&R, 2007).

Sande, Ken, *The Peacemaker* (Grand Rapids, MI: Baker, 2004).

Scott, Stuart, *The Exemplary Husband* (Bemidji, MN: Focus, revised edn. 2002).

Smith, Robert D., *The Christian Counselor's Medical Desk Reference* (Stanley, NC: Timeless Texts, 2000).

Tripp, Paul David, *War of Words* (Phillipsburg, NJ: P&R, 2000).

Welch, Edward T., *Addictions: A Banquet in the Grave* (Phillipsburg, NJ: P&R, 2001).

——*Blame It on the Brain?* (Phillipsburg, NJ: P&R, 1998).

——*When People Are Big and God Is Small* (Phillipsburg, NJ: P&R, 1997).

Whitney, Donald S., *Spiritual Disciplines for the Christian Life* (Colorado Springs, CO: NavPress, 1991).

——*Spiritual Disciplines within the Church* (Chicago: Moody Press, 1996).

## BOOKS TO STRENGTHEN PASTORAL MINISTRY

Adams, Jay E., *A Call to Discernment* (Eugene, OR: Harvest House, 1987).

——*Shepherding God's Flock* (Grand Rapids, MI: Zondervan, 1974).

Baxter, Richard, *The Reformed Pastor* (1656; 1974, Edinburgh: Banner of Truth).

Burroughs, Jeremiah, *Gospel Fear* (1647; 1991, Orlando, FL: Soli Deo Gloria).

Croft, Brian, ed., *The Practical Shepherding* series (Grand Rapids: Zondervan, 2014-15)

Dever, Mark, *Nine Marks of a Healthy Church* (Wheaton, IL: Crossway, 2004).

Duncan, J. Ligon, and Hunt, Susan, *Women's Ministry in the Local Church* (Wheaton, IL: Crossway, 2006).

Elliff, Tom, *A Passion for Prayer* (Wheaton, IL: Crossway, 1998).

Kuiper, R. B., *God-Centred Evangelism* (London: Banner of Truth, 1966).

Lloyd-Jones, D. Martyn, *What Is an Evangelical?* (Edinburgh: Banner of Truth, 1992).

MacArthur, John F., *The Master's Plan for the Church* (Chicago: Moody Press, 1991).

——and The Master's Seminary Faculty, *Rediscovering Pastoral Ministry* (Dallas: Word, 1995).

Murray, Iain, *Evangelicalism Divided* (Edinburgh: Banner of Truth, 2000).

Nettles, Thomas J., *By His Grace and For His Glory* (Lake Charles, LA: Cor Meum Tibi, 2002).

Piper, John, *Brothers, We are Not Professionals* (Nashville, TN: B&H, 2002).

——*Contending for Our All* (Wheaton, IL: Crossway, 2006).

Sanders, J. Oswald, *Spiritual Leadership* (Chicago: Moody Press, 1967).

Schreiner, Thomas R., *Paul: Apostle of God's Glory in Christ* (Downers Grove, IL: InterVarsity Press, 2001).

Shaw, John, *The Character of a Pastor according to God's Heart* (Ligonier, PA: Soli Deo Gloria, 1992).

Spurgeon, Charles H., *An All-Round Ministry* (Pasadena, TX: Pilgrim Publications, 1983).

Strauch, Alexander, *Biblical Eldership* (Littleton, CO: Lewis & Roth, 1986).

——*The New Testament Deacon* (Littleton, CO: Lewis & Roth, 1992).

Thomas, Curtis C., *Life in the Body of Christ* (Cape Coral, FL: Founders Press, 2006).

Watson, Thomas, *A Body of Divinity* (1692; 1965, London: Banner of Truth).

Webster, Douglas D., *Selling Jesus* (Downers Grove, IL: IVP, 1992).

Wells, David F., *The Courage to Be Protestant* (Grand Rapids, MI: Eerdmans, 2008).

——*God in the Wasteland* (Grand Rapids, MI: Eerdmans, 1994).

——*No Place for Truth* (Grand Rapids, MI: Eerdmans, 1993).

## BOOKS TO STRENGTHEN PREACHING

Braga, James, *How to Prepare Bible Messages* (Portland, OR: Multnomah, 1969).

Chappel, Bryan, *Christ-Centered Preaching* (Grand Rapids, MI: Baker, 2005).

Lawson, Steven J., *Famine in the Land* (Chicago: Moody Press, 2003).

MacArthur, John F., and The Master's Seminary Faculty, *Rediscovering Expository Preaching* (Dallas: Word, 1992).

Murray, David, *How Sermons Work* (Darlington, UK: Evangelical Press, 2011)

Murray, Iain, *Spurgeon v. Hyper-Calvinism* (Edinburgh: Banner of Truth, 1995).

Packer, J. I., *Evangelism and the Sovereignty of God* (Downers Grove, IL: InterVarsity Press, 1961).

Piper, John, *The Supremacy of God in Preaching* (Grand Rapids, MI: Baker, 1990).

Robinson, Haddon W., *Biblical Preaching* (Grand Rapids, MI: Baker, 1980).

Stott, John R. W., *Between Two Worlds* (Grand Rapids, MI: Eerdmans, 1982).

Wiersbe, Warren, and Perry, Lloyd M., *The Wycliffe Handbook of Preaching and Preachers* (Chicago: Moody Press, 1984).

## ELECTRONIC RESOURCES

Powlison, David, (ed.), *The Journal of Biblical Counseling on CD-ROM, Version 2.0.* (Glenside, PA: Christian Counseling & Educational Foundation, 1977–2005).

## WEBSITES WITH BIBLICAL COUNSELING RESOURCES

Association of Certified Biblical Counselors: www.biblicalcounseling.com

Christian Counseling & Educational Foundation: www.ccef.org

Counseling One Another: www.counselingoneanother.com

Faith Biblical Counseling: www.faithlafayette.org

Institute for Biblical Counseling and Discipleship: www.ibcd.org

Institute for Nouthetic Studies: www.nouthetic.org

Strengthening Ministries: www.mackministries.org

Women Helping Women: www.elysefitzpatrick.com

# ENDNOTES

## FOREWORD

1 This word is not restricted to and "does not mean the delivery of a learned and edifying or hortatory discourse in well-chosen words and a pleasant voice," Gerhard Kittel, Geoffrey W. Bromiley and Gerhard Friedrich, (eds.), *Theological Dictionary of the New Testament,* vol. iii (electronic edn; Grand Rapids, MI: Eerdmans, 1964–c.1976), p. 703.

## CHAPTER 1

1 David F. Wells, *No Place for Truth* (Grand Rapids, MI: Eerdmans, 1993), p. 177.

2 Cited in David F. Wells, *The Courage to Be Protestant* (Grand Rapids, MI: Eerdmans, 2008), p. 40.

3 Paul Tautges, *Counseling One Another* (Wapwallopen, PA: Shepherd Press, 2015).

4 William F. Arndt and F. Wilbur Gingrich, *A Greek-English Lexicon of the New Testament* (Chicago: University of Chicago Press, 1957), p. 684.

5 All italicized words or phrases within Scripture quotations indicate emphasis added by this author. Italics within non-Scriptural quotations are the original writer's.

6 http://www.gracegems.org/Ryle/m07.htm, accessed 10 May 2008.

7 Cited by John R. W. Stott, *Between Two Worlds* (Grand Rapids, MI: Eerdmans, 1982), p. 180.

## CHAPTER 2

1 Lance Quinn, "Discipling," in John MacArthur, (ed.), *Rediscovering Pastoral Ministry* (Dallas: Word, 1995), p. 334.

2 Robert G. Gromacki, *Stand Perfect in Wisdom* (Grand Rapids, MI: Baker, 1981), p. 81.

3 John Piper, *Let the Nations Be Glad* (Grand Rapids, MI: Baker, 1993), p. 94.

4 Patricia Souder, *Alex Leonovich: A Heart for the Soul of Russia* (Camp Hill, PA: Horizon, 1999), pp. 12–15.

5 William Brown, in Richard Baxter, *The Reformed Pastor* (1656; 1974, Edinburgh: Banner of Truth), p. 23.

6 Ibid., p. 176.

7 For a full explanation of the ministry of comforting one another, see Paul Tautges, *Comfort Those Who Grieve* (Leominster: Day One, 2009; ISBN: 978-1-84625-155-9).

8 Jerry Bridges, *Trusting God* (Colorado Springs, CO: NavPress, 1988), pp. 174–177.

9 Quoted in Iain Murray, *Spurgeon v. Hyper-Calvinism* (Edinburgh: Banner of Truth, 1995), p. 18.

10 Fritz Rienecker and Cleon Rogers, *A Linguistic Key to the Greek New Testament* (Grand Rapids, MI: Zondervan, 1976), p. 570.

11 Warren Wiersbe, *Real Worship* (Nashville, TN: Oliver Nelson, 1986), p. 165.

12 This key truth is fully developed in Paul Tautges, *Counseling One Another* (Wapwallopen, PA: Shepherd Press, 2015).

13 Quoted in J. Sidlow Baxter, *Explore the Book*, vol. vi (Grand Rapids, MI: Zondervan, 1960), p. 196.

14 Ibid., p. 200.

15 D. Martyn Lloyd-Jones, *What Is an Evangelical?* (Edinburgh: Banner of Truth, 1992), p. 45.

16 David Powlison, *Seeing with New Eyes* (Phillipsburg, NJ: P&R, 2003), p. 4.

17 Quoted in Baxter, *Explore the Book*, p. 201.

18 Rienecker and Rogers, *Linguistic Key*, p. 571.

19 Ibid., p. 602.

20 W. E. Vine, Merrill Unger, and William White, *Vine's Complete Expository Dictionary of Old and New Testament Words* (Nashville, TN: Thomas Nelson, 1985), p. 222.

21 Rienecker and Rogers, *Linguistic Key*, p. 602.

22 Baxter, *Reformed Pastor*, pp. 97–98.

23 James Strong, *Strong's Exhaustive Concordance of the Bible* (Peabody, MA: Hendricksen, n.d.), #472.

24 Richard Chenevix Trench, *Synonyms of the New Testament* (Grand Rapids, MI: Baker, 1989), p. 209.

25 Baxter, *Reformed Pastor*, p. 119.

26 Vine, Unger, and White, *Expository Dictionary*, p. 619.

27 Ibid., p. 180.

28 David F. Wells, *No Place for Truth, or, Whatever Happened to Evangelical Theology?* (Grand Rapids, MI: Eerdmans, 1993), p. 4.

29 Ibid., pp. 209–210.

30 Os Guiness, "America's Last Men and Their Magnificent Talking Cure," in *The Journal of Biblical Counseling,* 15/2 (1997), p. 23.

31 Gary Johnson, "Does Theology Still Matter?" in John Armstrong, (ed.), *The Coming Evangelical Crisis* (Chicago: Moody Press, 1996), p. 57.

32 Trench, *Synonyms,* p. 299.

33 Ibid., p. 90.

34 Ibid., p. 91.

35 Strong, *Concordance,* #2872.

36 Charles Bridges, *The Christian Ministry* (1830; 1967, Edinburgh: Banner of Truth), p. 67.

37 Rienecker and Rogers, *Linguistic Key,* p. 571.

38 D. A. Carson, *A Call to Spiritual Reformation* (Grand Rapids, MI: Baker, 1992), p. 211.

## CHAPTER 3

1 James Strong, *Strong's Exhaustive Concordance of the Bible* (Peabody, MA: Hendricksen, n.d.).

2 H. D. M. Spence, (ed.), *The Pulpit Commentary,* vol. xx (Grand Rapids, MI: Eerdmans, 1965), pp. 148–149.

3 W. E. Vine, Merrill Unger, and William White, *Vine's Complete Expository Dictionary of Old and New Testament Words* (Nashville, TN: Thomas Nelson, 1985), p. 493.

4 John F. MacArthur, *Ephesians* (MacArthur New Testament Commentary; Chicago: Moody Press, 1986), p. 143.

5 Fritz Rienecker and Cleon Rogers, *A Linguistic Key to the Greek New Testament* (Grand Rapids, MI: Zondervan, 1976), p. 531.

6 Ibid.

7 Kenneth S. Wuest, *Wuest's Word Studies: Ephesians* (Grand Rapids, MI: Eerdmans, 1953), p. 101.

8 John R. W. Stott, *Between Two Worlds* (Grand Rapids, MI: Eerdmans, 1982), p. 124.

9 John Shaw, *The Character of a Pastor According to God's Heart* (Ligonier, PA: Soli Deo Gloria, 1992), p. 13.

10 F. Wilbur Gingrich, *Shorter Lexicon of the Greek New Testament* (Chicago: University of Chicago Press, 1957), p. 418.

11 This ministry of compassionate confrontation is presented thoroughly in Paul Tautges, *Counseling One Another* (Wapwallopen, PA: Shepherd Press, 2015).

12 Richard Baxter, *The Reformed Pastor* (1656; 1974, Edinburgh: Banner of Truth), pp. 96–97.

13 Vine, Unger, and White, *Expository Dictionary,* p. 194.

14 Rienecker and Rogers, *Linguistic Key,* p. 531.

15 Vine, Unger, and White, *Expository Dictionary,* p. 348.

16 Rienecker and Rogers, *Linguistic Key,* p. 531.

17 W. Curtis Vaughan, *The Letter to the Ephesians* (Nashville, TN: Convention Press, 1963), p. 83.

18 Rienecker and Rogers, *Linguistic Key,* pp. 531–532.

19 William Hendricksen, *Galatians and Ephesians* (New Testament Commentary; Grand Rapids, MI: Baker, 1967), p. 202.

20 Vine, Unger, and White, *Expository Dictionary,* p. 137.

21 Steven J. Lawson, *Famine in the Land* (Chicago: Moody Press, 2003), p. 38.

22 D. Martyn Lloyd-Jones, *Christian Unity* (Grand Rapids, MI: Baker, 1980), pp. 241–242.

23 Spence, *Pulpit Commentary,* p. 160.

24 David Powlison, *Seeing with New Eyes* (Phillipsburg, NJ: P&R, 2003), pp. 5–6.

25 Vine, Unger, and White, *Expository Dictionary,* p. 242.

26 William F. Arndt and F. Wilbur Gingrich, *A Greek–English Lexicon of the New Testament* (Chicago: University of Chicago Press, 1957), p. 777.

27 Ibid.

28 Rienecker and Rogers, *Linguistic Key,* p. 632.

## CHAPTER 4

1 Louis A. Barbieri, *First and Second Peter* (Chicago: Moody Press, 1975), pp. 83–84.

2 Richard J. Goodrich and Albert L. Lukaszewski, *A Reader's Greek New Testament* (Grand Rapids, MI: Zondervan, 2003), p. 525.

3 Wayne Grudem, *1 Peter* (Tyndale New Testament Commentaries; Grand Rapids, MI: Eerdmans, 1988), p. 189.

4 Kenneth S. Wuest, *First Peter in the Greek New Testament* (Grand Rapids, MI: Eerdmans, 1942), p. 125.

5 J. Oswald Sanders, *Spiritual Leadership* (Chicago: Moody Press, 1967), p. 166.

6 Ibid., p. 33.

7 John R. W. Stott, *Between Two Worlds* (Grand Rapids, MI: Eerdmans, 1982), p. 284.

8 Quoted by Sanders, *Spiritual Leadership,* p. 180. Counseling One Another: A Theology of Interpersonal Discipleship

## COUNSELING ONE ANOTHER: A THEOLOGY OF INTERPERSONAL DISCIPLESHIP

Paul Tautges

A book to help believers understand the process of being transformed by God's grace and truth

Trade paperback, 192pp, ISBN 9781633420946

***"This book gets it right! Comprehensive and convincing, Counseling One Another shows how true biblical counseling and preaching fit hand-in-glove. Those who preach, teach or counsel regularly are sure to benefit greatly from this helpful resource."***

–Dr. John MacArthur, Pastor-Teacher, Grace Community Church; President, The Master's University and Seminary

***"Paul Tautges lays the theological foundation for biblical counseling–in a way that is both comprehensive and compassionate. This book demonstrates a staunch commitment to an expository, exegetical examination of counseling as presented in God's Word. Any pastor or lay person wanting a foundational starting point for understanding Christ-centered, comprehensive, and compassionate biblical counseling in the local church would be wise to read and reread Counseling One Another."***

–Bob Kellemen, Executive Director of The Biblical Counseling Coalition

## PRAY ABOUT EVERYTHING: CULTIVATING GOD-DEPENDENCY

Paul Tautges

An urgent call, with practical guidelines, for believers to commit themselves to regular and systematic heartfelt prayer as an essential spiritual discipline of the Christian life

Trade paperback, 128pp, ISBN 9781633421141

***"... a valuable contribution to our theology and practice of prayer."***

–Jerry Bridges, Best-selling author, "The Pursuit of Holiness"

***"... one of my favorite books on prayer."***

–Mark Dever, Senior Pastor, Capitol Hill Baptist Church, Washington, D.C., President, 9Marks

***"Use this book as a springboard to stimulate your own ideas on how you as a pastor or church leader can cultivate prayer in your church."***

–Joel R. Beeke, President, Puritan Reformed Theological Seminary, Grand Rapids, Michigan.

***"Paul Tautges has done a tremendous service to both pastors and church members with this little gem of a book."***

–Brian Croft, Senior Pastor, Auburndale Baptist Church, Louisville, Kentucky

***"Paul Tautges has produced this excellent resource for instructing and inspiring effectual prayer in the life of the local church. I highly recommend this book, not to be read, but read and implemented into the prayer life of your church family. It will be transforming!"***

–Daniel P. Fredericks, Church and Pastoral Ministries Consultant, IFCA International

HELP!
I'M CONFUSED ABOUT DATING
LIFELINE
joel james
SOMEONE I LOVE HAS BEEN ABUSED
I'M BEING DEPLOYED
MY TODDLER RULES THE HOUSE
HE'S STRUGGLING WITH PORNOGRAPHY
SOMEONE I LOVE HAS CANCER
I'M A SLAVE TO FOOD
I HAVE BREAST CANCER
MY SPOUSE HAS BEEN UNFAITHFUL
I WANT TO CHANGE
MY TEEN STRUGGLES WITH SAME-SEX ATTRACTIONS
I'M A SINGLE MOM
I CAN'T GET MOTIVATED
SHE'S STRUGGLING WITH PORNOGRAPHY
I'M DROWNING IN DEBT
I'M DEPRESSED
I'M LIVING WITH TERMINAL ILLNESS
I FEEL ASHAMED
MY TEEN IS REBELLIOUS
HELP!
MY KIDS ARE VIEWING PORNOGRAPHY
LIFELINE
tim challies
HELP!
I'VE BEEN TRAUMATIZED BY COMBAT
LIFELINE
barrett craig
SOMEONE I LOVE HAS ALZHEIMER'S
MY ANGER IS OUT OF CONTROL
I CAN'T FORGIVE
I WANT TO MODEL SUBMISSION IN MARRIAGE
I CAN'T HANDLE ALL THESE TRIALS
I'M IN A CONFLICT
I'M SO LONELY
MY FRIEND IS SUICIDAL
I NEED A CHURCH

## LIFELINE MINI-BOOKS

The LifeLine mini-books address day-to-day issues from a Bible-centered perspective, with an emphasis on bringing help and guidance to people who are struggling or suffering, as well as to those who minister to them.

Produced under the editorial direction of Dr. Paul Tautges, these resources include a clear gospel presentation, personal application projects, and a list of further resources.

Each mini-book is pocket sized (6 x 4 inches) and 64 pages in extent.

More info at www.lifelineminibooks.com.

***"These little books are directly targeted to the issues that we all face and they hit the bulls-eye. They are faithful to Scripture and demonstrate insight into its application. Churches need to make these available for their congregations."***

–John MacArthur, Pastor-Teacher, Grace Community Church; President, The Master's University and Seminary

***"These mini-books are exactly the kind of books you'd want to have available to you at church–short, biblical and inexpensive enough to give away.***

–Tim Challies, Blogger

***"They are on the cutting edge of what the Evangelical church needs today to advance God's work in our broken world."***

–Dr. Bob Kellemen, Chair of the Biblical Counseling and Discipleship Department, Crossroads Bible College

***"You can trust these resources to provide accessible, practical, and Bible-saturated help with many of the most common and perplexing problems found in our fallen world."***

–Dr. Heath Lambert, First Baptist Church, Jacksonville, FL, Executive Director the Association of Certified Biblical Counselors (ACBC)

*Help! He's Struggling with Pornography*, Brian Croft, 9781633420038

*Help! I Can't Forgive*, Jim Newcomer, 9781633420694

*Help! I Can't Get Motivated*, Adam Embry, 9781633420366

*Help! I Can't Handle All These Trials*, Joel James, 9781633420663

*Help! I Feel Ashamed*, Sue Nicewander, 9781633420571

*Help! I Have Breast Cancer*, Brenda Frields, 9781633420243

*Help! I Need a Church*, Jim Newheiser, 9781633420816

*Help! I Want to Change*, Jim Newheiser, 9781633420151

*Help! I Want to Model Submission in Marriage*, Glenda Hotton, 9781633420601

*Help! I'm a Single Mom*, Carol Trahan, 9781633420397

*Help! I'm a Slave to Food*, Sharon McCoy, 9781633420274

*Help! I'm Being Deployed*, Barrett Craig, 9781633420007

*Help! I'm Confused About Dating*, Joel James, 9781633420427

*Help! I'm Depressed*, Carol Trahan, 9781633420519

*Help! I'm Drowning in Debt*, John Temple, 9781633420458

*Help! I'm in a Conflict*, Ernie Baker, 9781633420786

*Help! I'm Living With Terminal Illness*, Reggie Weems, 9781633420540

*Help! I'm So Lonely*, Deborah Howard, 9781633421158

*Help! I've Been Traumatized by Combat*, Barrett Craig, 9781633421035

*Help! My Anger Is Out of Control*, Jim Newheiser, 9781633420724

*Help! My Friend Is Suicidal*, Bruce Ray, 9781633420755

*Help! My Kids Are Viewing Pornography*, Tim Challies, 9781633421271

*Help! My Spouse Has Been Unfaithful*, Mike Summers, 9781633420182

*Help! My Teen is Rebellious*, Dave & Judi Coats, 9781633420489

*Help! My Teen Struggles with Same-sex Attraction*, Ben Marshall, 9781633420304

*Help! My Toddler Rules the House*, Paul & Karen Tautges, 9781633420090

*Help! She's Struggling with Pornography*, Rachel Coyle, 9781633420335

*Help! Someone I Love Has Alzheimer's*, Deborah Howard, 9781633420632

*Help! Someone I Love Has Been Abused*, Jim Newheiser, 9781633420069

*Help! Someone I Love Has Cancer*, Deborah Howard, 9781633420120

# COUNSEL FOR THE HEART

## A RESOURCE for WORD-BASED TRANSFORMATION and PRACTICAL DISCIPLESHIP